W9-ABZ-416

FIVE HUNDRED COPIES

OF THE FIRST EDITION OF

SIXES AND SEVENS

HAVE BEEN SIGNED BY

THE AUTHOR

Robert Manson Myers

CHRISTMAS 2004

SIXES AND SEVENS

Books by Robert Manson Myers

HANDEL'S MESSIAH: A TOUCHSTONE OF TASTE (1948)
(New Edition, 1971)

FROM BEOWULF TO VIRGINIA WOOLF (1952)
(New Edition, Revised, 1984)

HANDEL, DRYDEN, AND MILTON (1956)

RESTORATION COMEDY (1961)

THE CHILDREN OF PRIDE (1972)
(New Edition, Abridged, 1984)

A GEORGIAN AT PRINCETON (1976)

QUINTET (1991)

SIXES AND SEVENS (2004)

Portrait by J.D. Fergusson

SIXES AND SEVENS

Scenes from a Marriage

A Comic Trilogy
Drawn from the Novels of
Ada Leverson

by
ROBERT MANSON MYERS

Charlotte
JOSTENS BOOKS
2004

PS
3563
.Y455
S58
2004

Copyright © 2004 by Robert Manson Myers
Manufactured in the United States of America

LCCN: 2004-110572
ISBN: 0-9759530-0-1

FIRST EDITION

CAUTION
Professionals and amateurs are hereby warned that these plays,
being fully protected under the copyright laws of the United
States of America, the British Commonwealth, including Canada,
and all other countries subscribing to the Berne and Universal
Copyright Conventions, are subject to royalty. All rights, including professional, amateur, motion picture, recitation, lecturing,
public reading, radio and television broadcasting, and translation
into foreign languages, are strictly reserved. All inquiries concern-
ing rights should be addressed to the publisher.

JOSTENS BOOKS
2400 Crownpoint Executive Drive
Charlotte, North Carolina 28227

56958545

In Memoriam

MATILDA MANSON WYNN
(MRS. HORWOOD PRETTYMAN MYERS)
18 AUGUST 1892
30 DECEMBER 1962

He shall deliver thee in six troubles:
Yea, in seven there shall no evil touch thee.

JOB 5:19

CONTENTS

Preface

ADA LEVERSON (1862-1933), journalist, drama critic, and novelist, is perhaps best known for her courageous support of Oscar Wilde at the time of his public disgrace. To Wilde she was "The Sphinx"—"the wittiest woman in the world." Her brilliant circle included Henry James, George Moore, John Singer Sargent, George Bernard Shaw, Walter Sickert, Max Beerbohm, Aubrey Beardsley, Ronald Firbank, William Walton, and the three Sitwells (Edith, Osbert, and Sacheverell). Her pieces in *Punch* and *The Yellow Book* and her dramatic criticism in *The Saturday Review* delighted *fin-de-siècle* readers at home and abroad. And her six sparkling novels of manners—*The Twelfth Hour* (1907), *Love's Shadow* (1908), *The Limit* (1911), *Tenterhooks* (1912), *Bird of Paradise* (1914), and *Love at Second Sight* (1916)—satirized with charm and sly wit the Edwardian social scene.

Since Ada Leverson was a friend of dramatists and herself a drama critic, it seems peculiarly fitting that her novels, all vividly scenic, be adapted for the stage. *Sixes and Sevens,* a comic trilogy, embraces the three novels delineating the marriage of Edith and Bruce Ottley. *Lover Pro Tem,* virtually a succession of drawing-room sketches, anticipates the marital tensions to follow in *Tenterhooks* and *Love at Second Sight.* The portrait of Edith Ottley is undoubtedly a self-portrait of Ada Leverson; the portrait of Bruce Ottley is as surely a portrait of her estranged husband, Ernest Leverson.

Each of the three plays comprising *Sixes and Sevens* may be performed independently of the other two; the three plays performed as a cycle achieve a cumulative whole. The sequence of scenes in each act should be continuous: the pause between scenes should be as brief as possible. It is suggested that the opening of each act and the transition from scene to scene be accompanied by appropriate salon ("palm court") music—light classics evoking the mood of Edwardian England: elegant, gracious, lively, bittersweet.

ROBERT MANSON MYERS

SIXES AND SEVENS

Lover Pro Tem

Lover Pro Tem, a comedy in two acts, is drawn from the novel *Love's Shadow,* by Ada Leverson, first published in London in 1908.

CHARACTERS

BRUCE OTTLEY

EDITH OTTLEY

BENNETT

MR. RAGGETT

ARCHIE OTTLEY

MRS. OTTLEY

SCENES

Time: 1908

Place: London

The scene is set in the drawing room of the
Ottley flat in Linden Mansions, Cadogan Square

ACT ONE

Scene 1   Morning

Scene 2   Evening

Scene 3   Afternoon

Scene 4   Early evening

Scene 5   Afternoon

ACT TWO

Scene 1   Afternoon

Scene 2   Evening

Scene 3   Morning

Scene 4   Early evening

Scene 5   Morning

Act One

Scene One

The drawing room of the Ottley flat in Linden Mansions, Cadogan Square, London. Morning. It is a comfortable, pleasant, informal room agreeably furnished. A fire is burning on the hearth.

At rise BRUCE *and* EDITH OTTLEY *are seated at a small breakfast table near the window.* BRUCE, *aged twenty-nine, tall, good-looking, well built, with a thin moustache, is reading a newspaper.* EDITH, *aged twenty-seven, intelligent, charming, and very pretty, is pouring coffee.*

BRUCE (*from behind his newspaper*): Edith, dear.

EDITH (*sweetly*): Yes, Bruce?

BRUCE (*still behind his newspaper*): There's one thing I really must implore you.

EDITH: Yes, Bruce?

BRUCE (*putting down his newspaper*): Please don't make me late again at the office!

EDITH: Certainly not, Bruce.

BRUCE (*rising from the table*): Now I must write that letter before I go.

EDITH: Of course, Bruce.

BRUCE (*going to the writing table*): Why didn't I write it last night?

EDITH: I can't think, Bruce.

BRUCE (*sitting down at the writing table*): How many g's in "Raggett"?

EDITH: In *what?*

BRUCE (*beginning to write*): In "Raggett." (*Sharply*) How absurd you are!

EDITH: Why, Bruce!

BRUCE: It's a curious thing—with all the fuss about higher education nowadays, girls are not even taught to spell.

EDITH: It *is* curious, isn't it? But even if I *had* been taught to spell, I might just not have been taught to spell "Raggett." It's a name, isn't it?

BRUCE: It's a very well-known name.

EDITH: I daresay it is, but I don't know it.

BRUCE: Ah—you don't know it.

EDITH (*brightly*): Would you like to see Archie before you go?

BRUCE: What a question! I always like to see Archie. But you know perfectly well, Edith, I haven't time for the boy this morning. (*He finishes his letter and returns to the breakfast table.*)

EDITH: Very well, dear. You can see him this afternoon.

BRUCE: Why do you say that? You know perfectly well I'm playing golf this afternoon. It really is sad, Edith, when a man has to work so hard he scarcely has time for his wife and child…. What are *you* doing today?

EDITH: Hyacinth's coming to fetch me for a drive in the motor.

BRUCE: I'm so glad, darling, you have such a delightful friend—when I can't be with you. I admire Hyacinth very much. And she seems devoted to you, which is really very nice of her. What I mean is, in her position she might know anybody. You see my point?

EDITH: Quite.

BRUCE: How did you meet her originally?

EDITH: We were school friends.

BRUCE: She's such a lovely creature I wonder she doesn't marry.

EDITH: Yes, but *she* has to find someone *she* thinks a lovely creature too.

BRUCE: Edith, dear.

EDITH: Yes, Bruce?

BRUCE: I wish you wouldn't snap me up like that. Oh, I know you don't mean it, but it's growing on you, rather.

EDITH: Is it really?

BRUCE: You don't mind my mentioning it, do you?

EDITH: Not at all, dear. (*Suddenly remembering*) Oh, Bruce, you won't forget we're dining with your people tonight.

BRUCE: Good heavens! What a nuisance!

EDITH: Oh, Bruce!

BRUCE: It's such an infernally long way.

EDITH: It's only to Kensington.

BRUCE: *West* Kensington. It's off the map! I'm not an explorer—I don't pretend to be. And it's not only the frightful distance and the frightful expense of getting there, but when I *do* get there— Do you consider that my people treat me with proper deference?

EDITH: With proper *what?*

BRUCE: Deference. I admit I like deference. I need it. And at my people's—well, frankly, I don't get it.

EDITH: If you need it, dear, I hope you get it. But remember—they *are* your father and mother.

BRUCE: What do you mean by that?

EDITH: I mean—they know you very well.

BRUCE: Do you imply—?

EDITH: Oh, no, Bruce, of course I don't. But really I think your people are charming.

BRUCE: To *you* I know they are. You and my mother can talk about Archie and his nurse and housekeeping and fashions, and it's all very jolly for *you*. But where's the fun for a man of the world?

EDITH: Your father—

BRUCE: My father! I don't mind telling you, Edith, I don't consider my father a man of the world. Good heavens, when we're alone together, what do you suppose he talks about? He complains! Finds fault, if you please! Says I don't work. Makes out I'm extravagant. Have *you* ever found me extravagant?

EDITH: No, dear. I'm sure you've never been extravagant—to *me.*

BRUCE: He's not on *my* level intellectually in any way. I doubt very much if he's capable of understanding me at all. Still, I suppose we might as well go and get it over. (*Shaking his head*) My people's dinners are really an awful bore.

EDITH: How would you like it if some day Archie were to call us "my people" and talk about *us* the way you talk about yours?

BRUCE: Good heavens, if Archie ever treats *me* with any want of deference, I'll cut him off with a shilling!

EDITH (*laughing*): Oh, do give me the shilling now!

BRUCE: I suppose they don't expect *us* to ask *them*. I daresay it's well known we can't return all the hospitality we receive.

EDITH: I daresay it is. (*Suddenly remembering*) Oh, Bruce, I *do* wish you'd be an angel and let me have a little cash to go to Naylor & Rope's. There are some marvellous bargains—spring novelties. And Archie absolutely *needs* one or two things.

BRUCE: I object to spring sales. Women buy a lot of things they don't want, and ruin their husbands under the ridiculous impression they're buying bargains.

EDITH: I won't ruin you, dear. I want to get Archie a coat and a hat. (*Watching BRUCE's expression*) I only want a sovereign or two. (*She smiles brightly and passes BRUCE the toast.*)

BRUCE (*relenting*): Well, dear, you know I'm not a rich man, don't you?

EDITH: Yes, dear.

BRUCE: But I'd much prefer that you get Archie's things at a first-rate place like Wears & Swells, where we have an account.

EDITH: Of course, dear, if you like. But it'll cost more.

BRUCE: Then that's settled. And now I want to speak to you of my friend Raggett.

EDITH: Your friend Raggett.

BRUCE: You don't know Raggett, but I think you'll like him. I *think* you will. In any case, there's no doubt Raggett's been remarkably decent to me. In fact, he's a very good sort.

EDITH: Fancy!

BRUCE: Why do you say "Fancy"?

EDITH: I don't exactly know. I suppose I *must* say *something*. I'm sure he's nice if he's a friend of yours, dear.

BRUCE: He's a clever chap in his way. When I say "clever," I don't mean clever in the ordinary sense.

EDITH: I see.

BRUCE: He's very amusing. He said a very funny thing to me the other day. Very funny indeed. But it's no use repeating it; you wouldn't understand.... Perhaps after all I'd better ask him to dine at the club.

EDITH: Oh, no, Bruce! Let him come here. Don't you think I'm worthy to see Raggett?

BRUCE: Oh, nonsense, dear! I'm very proud of you. Mind you, Raggett's quite a man of the world. And yet he *isn't* a man of the world, if you know what I mean.

EDITH: I see.

BRUCE (*suddenly*): I've very nearly made up my mind to have Raggett to dinner at the Savoy.

EDITH: At the Savoy!

BRUCE (*looking around the room with marked disdain*): No doubt this little flat is very comfortable. And Cook, thanks to you, isn't half bad. But one can't give *dinners* here! And after all I've said to Raggett—oh, one thing and another—I fancy I've given him the impression of something rather luxurious. It won't matter if he calls here in the afternoon some day. But for a man like that I'd rather—yes—the Savoy.... You look as if you objected.

EDITH: Not at all, dear! It'll be rather fun. I'm so glad you can afford it. We haven't an account there, you know.

BRUCE: Well, I propose to make a slight sacrifice for once. Women never understand that to do things well, once in a way, is sometimes a—a very good thing.

EDITH: Oh, I *am* getting curious to see Raggett!

BRUCE: My dear Edith, he's nothing particular to *see*. But he's a man who might be very useful.

EDITH: Will you take a private room?

BRUCE: I think not. But, Edith, dear, I'll want you to look nice. What will you wear?

EDITH: I think I'll wear—My Other Dress.

BRUCE: Is it all right?

EDITH: It ought to be. I've cut the point into a square, and taken four yards out of the skirt, and made the chiffon off my wedding dress into kimono sleeves, and turned the pointed waistband round, so that it's quite short-waisted at the back, and—

BRUCE: Oh, don't tell me all the horrible details! I think you might take a little interest in *me*.

EDITH: Why, yes, Bruce.

BRUCE: *I* thought of wearing a buttonhole.

EDITH: A buttonhole!

BRUCE: Though you may have forgotten it now, Edith, before I was a dull old married man I was supposed to dress rather well.

EDITH: I know you were, dear.

BRUCE: I thought I'd wear a white carnation.

EDITH: I should wear *two*—one each side. It would be more striking.

BRUCE: That's right—make fun of me!

EDITH: Oh, Bruce!

BRUCE: It's awful not having a valet.

EDITH: But it would be even worse if we had. Where on earth could we put him? In the bathroom?

BRUCE (*rising from the table*): Now, Edith, dear, do tell Cook we're dining out. She might have a holiday tonight. And tell her I hope to find the omelette less leathery tomorrow.

EDITH: Bruce, dear—

BRUCE: And now I must go. (*At the door*) Yes, Edith, you can take it from me, once for all: *Raggett's all right*. (*Checking his watch*) Good heavens, Edith! You've made me late again at the office! (*He rushes out.*)

CURTAIN

Scene Two

Evening. EDITH *is seated on the sofa knitting;* BRUCE *is seated in a chair reading a book.*

EDITH: Fancy!

BRUCE (*putting down his book*): Fancy what?

EDITH: Somehow I never should have thought it.

BRUCE: Never should have thought what? You have a way, Edith, of assuming I know the end of your story before I've heard the beginning.

EDITH: I shouldn't have been so surprised if they'd been anywhere else. But just *there.*

BRUCE: Who? Where?

EDITH: Perhaps I'd better not tell you. (*She gets up to ring the bell.*)

BRUCE: No! Don't ring! I don't want Bennett to witness a painful scene.

EDITH: A painful scene!

BRUCE: Naturally, Edith, I'm distressed at your conduct.

EDITH: Conduct!

BRUCE: Don't echo my words, Edith! Naturally I'm hurt at your keeping things from me. Your own husband! I may have my faults— (EDITH *nods.*) I may have my faults—but I don't deserve this.

EDITH: Oh, Bruce, I was only thinking I'm sorry if I was irritating. I'll tell you.

BRUCE: Go on.

EDITH: When Nurse and Archie were out in the Gardens this morning, *who* do you think they met?

BRUCE: This is not a game. I'm not going to guess. You seem to take me for a child.

EDITH: Well, you won't tell anybody, will you?

BRUCE: That depends. I'm making no promises beforehand.

EDITH: Well, then, I'll trust you.

BRUCE: Thanks! I should think you *would!*

EDITH: Nurse and Archie met Hyacinth Verney walking with Cecil Reeve in Kensington Gardens. They weren't walking.

BRUCE: Then why did you say they were?

EDITH: It's the same thing. They were sitting down.

BRUCE: How *can* it be the same thing?

EDITH: They were sitting down under a tree, and Nurse saw them *holding hands.*

BRUCE (*horrified*): Holding hands!

EDITH: Holding hands. I can't help thinking they must be engaged. Isn't it extraordinary Hyacinth hasn't told me! What do you think?

BRUCE: I don't know *what* to think! I'm surprised. I'm pained. A girl like Hyacinth, a friend of yours, behaving like a housemaid out with a soldier in the open street!

EDITH: It wasn't the street, Bruce.

BRUCE: It's the same idea.

EDITH: A quiet part of the Gardens.

BRUCE: That makes it even worse! (*Considering*) Well! After what you've told me, I scarcely think I can allow you to go out with Hyacinth tomorrow.

EDITH: Oh, Bruce! How can you be so absurd? I *must* go. I want to hear all about it!

BRUCE: Have I ever objected to your great intimacy with Hyacinth Verney? Have I? But now—now—I'm utterly deceived in her.

EDITH: Deceived!

BRUCE: Don't repeat my words, Edith. I won't have it! Certainly I'm deceived. I thought Hyacinth was a fitting companion for you. I *thought* so.

EDITH: Oh, Bruce—really! Where's the harm? Perhaps they're

engaged. And if they are I think it's charming. Cecil is such a nice, amusing, good-looking boy, and—

BRUCE: *I* formed *my* opinion of Cecil Reeve some time ago.

EDITH: You only met him once.

BRUCE: Once is *more* than enough for me to form a judgement. He's absolutely worthless. He knows nothing about anything. I found *that* out when we were smoking after dinner. But *her* conduct I regard as infinitely worse. I always imagined she was respectably brought up—a lady!

EDITH: Good gracious! Anyone can see *that!* She's the most charming girl in the world!

BRUCE: *Outwardly,* no doubt, she *seems* all right. But now you see what she really is. Such behaviour would be dreadful enough in private. But in public! Think of the example!

EDITH (*laughing*): The example, you mean, to Archie?

BRUCE: Don't laugh, Edith. This is no laughing matter. Certainly to Archie—to anyone.... Now, I've only one thing to say.

EDITH: Do say it.

BRUCE: I never wish to hear Hyacinth Verney's name mentioned again. You are never to speak of her to me. Do you hear?

EDITH: Yes, Bruce.

BRUCE: I'm shocked—I'm horrified—to find Hyacinth Verney a snake in the grass.

EDITH: Oh, I'm sure she didn't look a bit like a snake in the grass. She wore that lovely grey dress and a hat with roses.

BRUCE: How do *you* know? Did *Archie* tell you? No! You lowered yourself to question Nurse! A nice opinion Nurse must have of your friends now!... Well, *that's* over! I won't blame *you,* dear, but I must never hear anything more about Hyacinth. (*Suddenly*) *Why is there no coffee?*

EDITH: Oh—you said I wasn't to ring. (*She rings the bell.*)

BRUCE (*in a high, condescending voice*): Have you seen that interesting article in the evening paper, dear, about the solicitor general?

EDITH: The solicitor general?

BRUCE: Read it. Read it and improve your mind. Far better for a woman to make herself intellectually a companion for her husband—are you listening?—than to be always gossiping about people and their paltry private affairs.

EDITH: Yes, dear.

(BENNETT, *the maid, enters bringing coffee*. EDITH *pours;* BENNETT *hands the cup to* BRUCE, *then goes out*.)

BRUCE: In what direction did you say they were going?

EDITH: They were going in the opposite direction.

BRUCE: Opposite to what? Now, that's the difference between a woman's intellect and a man's. You can't be logical! What do you mean by "opposite"?

EDITH: Why, Bruce, I mean just *opposite*. The other way.

BRUCE: Do you mean they walked off separately?

EDITH: Oh, *no!* They were going away together, and looking so happy…. But really, Bruce, I'm sorry I bothered you. I had no idea you'd feel it so much.

BRUCE: *Feel* it! Of course I feel it! I'm distressed to find that a wife of mine is intimate with people like that. (EDITH *rises and goes to the writing table*.) Where are you going?

EDITH: I'm writing Hyacinth I can't go out with her tomorrow.

BRUCE: Why can't you go out with her?

EDITH: You said I was never to see her again.

BRUCE: Yes—but don't be in a hurry. Since you wish it so much, I'll permit you to go out with her this once—for the last time, of course—so that you can find out if she really *is* engaged to that young ass. What a mercenary scoundrel he must be!

EDITH: Oh, Bruce—*anyone* would admire Hyacinth! And Cecil's very well off himself.

BRUCE: Do you consider *that* to his credit? So should *I* be well off if I had relations who died and left me a lot of money. Don't defend him, Edith; his conduct is simply disgraceful. What right has he to expect to marry a beautiful girl like Hyacinth? Good gracious, does he want everything?

EDITH: I suppose—he likes her.

BRUCE: That's not particularly clever of him. So would any man. What I object to most about that empty-headed cad is he's never satisfied. He wants the earth!

EDITH: Really, Bruce, one would think you were quite—

BRUCE: Quite what?

EDITH: Well, quite jealous of him, to hear you talk.

BRUCE: The incident is now closed. We'll never discuss it again.

EDITH: Very well, dear.

BRUCE: What *I* don't understand is how old Sir Charles Cannon can allow his ward to be tearing about all over London with a man of Reeve's antecedents.

EDITH: What's the matter with his antecedents? I didn't know he had any.

BRUCE: Don't interrupt. And Miss Stewart? Where was Miss Stewart, I'd like to know?

EDITH: I can't *think*.

BRUCE: A nice way *she* does her duty as chaperone!

EDITH: Bruce, dear, Hyacinth's twenty-three. She's not a child. Miss Stewart's her companion; but she can't follow Hyacinth about if she doesn't wish it.

BRUCE: She *should* wish it. Do you think Sir Charles knows of these goings-on?

EDITH: I shouldn't think he knows the details.

BRUCE: Then isn't it my duty as a married man and father of a family to communicate with him on the subject?

EDITH: Perhaps you'd better, Bruce, if you really feel it your duty. Personally, of course, I'd rather you didn't.

BRUCE (*suddenly*): No! No! I won't do anything of the sort! Is it *my* business to open her guardian's eyes? No! Let them go their own way. Do you hear, Edith? Let them do whatever they please.

EDITH: Yes, Bruce—I was going to.

BRUCE: Mind you, they'll be wretched.

EDITH: Why do you think they'll be wretched?

BRUCE: Of course they will! People who behave that way before—

EDITH: Why, Bruce, dear, *we* used to sit in the garden.

BRUCE: Of course—after your father had given his consent.

EDITH: And once or twice before.

BRUCE: Don't compare the two cases. *I* was a man of the world. At first your father didn't seem to like me, but I reasoned with him. I always reason calmly with people. And then he came round. Do you remember how pleased you were that day?

EDITH: Then why be so severe?

BRUCE: You don't understand, Edith, how it jars on me to think of any friend of yours behaving in a manner that's— Are you sure they're engaged?

EDITH: I'm not at *all* sure they're engaged!

BRUCE: Well, of course, if they don't marry now after what Archie saw, it'll be a public scandal, that's all I can say.

EDITH: What do you propose?

BRUCE: I don't quite know. I must think it over.... Look here, Edith—if you don't mind, I think I'll go for a stroll. The flat seems so hot tonight.

EDITH: Oh, Bruce!

BRUCE: I *must* go, dear. I feel the need of air.

EDITH: Oh, Bruce—you won't be long?

BRUCE: I *might* go down to the club for half an hour. I'll see. Good night, dear.

EDITH: Good night, Bruce.

BRUCE (*at the door*): What were Nurse's exact words?

EDITH: She said: "Miss Verney seemed to be carrying on anyhow with a young gentleman in Kensington Gardens." And then she said it was Mr. Reeve.

BRUCE: Disgusting! Horrible! (*He goes out, shaking his head.*)

CURTAIN

Scene Three

Afternoon. EDITH *is seated at the piano, playing a sentimental tune.* BENNETT *enters bringing a vase of flowers.*

BENNETT: If you please, ma'am, a gentleman called and left these flowers.

EDITH (*rising from the piano*): Who was it, Bennett?

BENNETT: He wouldn't give his name, ma'am. There's a note for you.

EDITH (*taking the note*): Thank you, Bennett. (BENNETT *places the flowers on the table and goes out.* EDITH *opens the note and reads.*) "Dear Mrs. Ottley, I went for a bicycle ride yesterday afternoon and plucked these flowers for you. If you have a moment, I wonder if you'd let me call. Sincerely yours, F.J. Raggett. P.S. I'm extremely busy, but I'm free at any time. Perhaps tomorrow might suit you? Or if you're engaged tomorrow, perhaps today? I'd ask you to ring me up and let me know, but I'm not on the telephone."

(BENNETT *returns.*)

BENNETT: It's the gentleman that left the flowers, ma'am, and could you see him for a minute?

EDITH: Certainly, Bennett.

(BENNETT *goes to the entrance hall and returns with* MR. RAGGETT. *He is a shy, uncomfortable, shabby-looking man in his mid-thirties.*)

BENNETT (*announcing*): Mr. Raggett! (*She goes out.*)

EDITH (*in her sweetest voice*): Why, Mr. Raggett! How very kind of you to come and see me! And these lovely flowers! They quite brighten one up!

MR. RAGGETT: I'm glad you think they're all right.

EDITH: They're beautiful! Fancy your plucking them all yourself! Where did you find these lilies? I always fancied they were hothouse plants.

MR. RAGGETT: Oh, I was bicycling. I just saw them, you know. I thought you might like them…. How is Ottley?

EDITH: Bruce is very well, thank you. Haven't you seen him lately?

MR. RAGGETT: Not really. I've been working so fearfully hard at the British Museum. I don't run up against Ottley much at the British Museum.

EDITH: No—I suppose not. (*An uneasy pause.*) Won't you have some tea?

MR. RAGGETT: No, thank you. I never take it. (*Another uneasy pause. Then they speak at the same time.*)

EDITH: Have you been—?

MR. RAGGETT: Do you know—?

EDITH: Oh, I beg your pardon.

MR. RAGGETT: Oh, I beg yours.

EDITH: Do say what you were going to say.

MR. RAGGETT: Oh, please finish your sentence.

EDITH: I wasn't going to say anything.

MR. RAGGETT: Nor was I. (*Another uneasy pause.*)

EDITH: I was going to ask if you'd been to the Savoy lately.

MR. RAGGETT: Oh, no, Mrs. Ottley—I've only been there once in my life. It was a great event for me.

EDITH: Really?

MR. RAGGETT: I met my ideal there. (*He fixes on* EDITH *an ardent but respectful stare. She smiles.*) I'm afraid I'm not amusing you much, Mrs. Ottley. I wasn't brought up in a very amusing atmosphere. I don't think I ever heard a joke till quite recently.

EDITH: Really?

MR. RAGGETT: My father would sometimes say at night, "Now it's time for Bedfordshire." But I wasn't amused at *that* after I was ten years old.

EDITH: But surely—

MR. RAGGETT: My family are really very serious. I should never dream of asking them even a riddle.

EDITH: Did you say you heard a joke recently?

MR. RAGGETT (*blushing and looking down*): I'm very sorry, Mrs. Ottley, but I'm afraid I can't tell you. It isn't suited to your—well, to your *atmosphere.*

EDITH: Oh, *really,* Mr. Raggett! Can't you *arrange* it?

MR. RAGGETT: Impossible. Quite impossible.

EDITH (*changing the subject*): Do you go much to the theatre?

MR. RAGGETT: Never. It would interfere with my work.

EDITH: What *is* your work, exactly?

MR. RAGGETT: It's difficult to explain, Mrs. Ottley. It takes a great many forms.

EDITH: Oh, yes?

MR. RAGGETT: Just at this moment I'm a Legitimist.

EDITH: A *what?*

MR. RAGGETT: A Legitimist. We put violets on the statue of King Charles the Martyr in February.

EDITH: Ah! That must be very hard work.

MR. RAGGETT: Oh, it isn't only that. I'm a kind of secretary, you see, to the society.

EDITH: Really? What fun it must be! Can I belong?

MR. RAGGETT: Oh, dear, yes, of course, Mrs. Ottley. If you like.

EDITH: What should I have to do?

MR. RAGGETT: Well, first of all you'd have to pay a shilling.

EDITH: Yes?

MR. RAGGETT: And then you'd be eligible for a year's probation.

EDITH: And what should I do after that?

MR. RAGGETT: Well, after that, you see, you'd have to bide your time.

EDITH: That doesn't sound very hard. Just pay a shilling and bide your time.

MR. RAGGETT: Do you really think you'd care to join?

EDITH: Oh, yes—yes. I always hated Oliver Cromwell.

MR. RAGGETT: But that alone, I'm afraid, would hardly be— You see, there might be a revolution at any moment.

EDITH: A revolution! But—excuse my asking you—what has that to do with the British Museum?

MR. RAGGETT: I can hardly tell you offhand like this, Mrs. Ottley. But if you let me come again one day—

EDITH: Oh, certainly! Do come again.

MR. RAGGETT: Then I'll say good-bye for today. I—I hope I haven't trespassed on your valuable—

EDITH: Oh, no—not in the least.

MR. RAGGETT (*lingering*): I've enjoyed our talk so much.

EDITH (*kindly*): So have I, Mr. Raggett. It's been most interesting.

MR. RAGGETT: I felt—I somehow felt there was a kind of—may I say, *sympathy*.

EDITH: Quite so.

MR. RAGGETT (*proffering his hand*): Well, good-bye, Mrs. Ottley.

EDITH: Good-bye, Mr. Raggett.

MR. RAGGETT (*at the door*): Give my kind regards to Ottley! (*He goes out, leaving* EDITH *smiling quizzically.*)

CURTAIN

Scene Four

Early evening. EDITH *is seated at the writing table, pen in hand.* BRUCE *enters.*

EDITH (*looking up*): Oh, hello, darling. Did you have a nice day?

BRUCE (*sourly*): A nice day!

EDITH (*rising from the writing table*): What do you think Archie brought home today in his Noah's ark?

BRUCE: I can't think.

EDITH: Two snails!

BRUCE: Two snails! *How* revolting! I don't know *where* Archie gets his tastes. Not from *my* family; *that* I know!

EDITH: Fancy, Bruce—Raggett called today.

BRUCE (*suddenly incensed*): *Who?*

EDITH: Raggett.

BRUCE: *Raggett?* You mean to say Raggett came here?

EDITH: Yes, dear. He paid a visit.

BRUCE: *Raggett paid a visit here?*

EDITH: Why shouldn't he, Bruce?

BRUCE: I don't know, but it seems very odd.

EDITH: Odd?

BRUCE: Raggett never pays visits…. What did he think of the flat?

EDITH: He didn't say. He talked about his work.

BRUCE: How did he seem?

EDITH: He seemed vague. Quite good-natured, but vague. Fancy his bringing me all those flowers!

BRUCE: *He* brought you *flowers? Raggett?*

EDITH: Surely you don't mind?

BRUCE (*smouldering*): We'll talk it over after dinner.

EDITH (*pleasantly, changing the subject*): I saw Hyacinth today.

BRUCE: Ah! What news of Hyacinth and Cecil?

EDITH: They seem very happy.

BRUCE: Happy! *That* can't last. (*He looks fiercely at the flowers.*) Now, Edith, what's the meaning of all this? Mind, I'm not jealous. It's not in my nature to be jealous. What I dislike is being made a fool of. If I thought Raggett, after all I've done for him—

EDITH: Oh, Bruce! How can you be so absurd? A poor harmless creature—

BRUCE: Harmless creature indeed! I think it extremely marked—calling on you when I was out.

EDITH: He didn't *know* you were out. It's the usual time to pay a visit, and he really came just to ask me to join the society.

BRUCE: I don't call Raggett a society man.

EDITH: He's a *secret*-society man. He wants me to become a Legitimist.

BRUCE: A *what?*

EDITH: A Legitimist.

BRUCE (*striking the table with his fist*): Now, Edith, I won't have any nonsense of that sort here! Goodness knows where it will end! Soon he'll be asking you to join the suffragettes!

EDITH: Why, Bruce!

BRUCE: I think I'll write Raggett.

EDITH: Oh, Bruce!

BRUCE: I'll write Raggett and tell him you complained to me.

EDITH: Bruce—

BRUCE: I'll tell him I won't have these constant visits and marked attentions to my wife.

EDITH: Bruce—

BRUCE: I'll ask him to keep his secret societies to himself, and not to interfere with the peace and harmony of a happy English home. (*He goes to the writing table and prepares to write.*)

EDITH: Oh, Bruce, I'm sure he didn't mean the slightest harm. He thought it was the proper thing, after dining with us.

BRUCE: But it isn't *like* the man, Edith! It isn't Raggett! He's no slave to convention. I can't help fancying there must have been some ulterior motive. It seems to me sinister. That's the word—*sinister.*

EDITH: Would you think it sinister if he never came here again?

BRUCE: Well, perhaps not. But in allowing this to pass—isn't it the thin edge of the wedge?

EDITH: Give him a chance and see. Don't be in a hurry. After all, he's your great friend. And what's he done? Brought a few flowers and called here once. I'm sure he thought you'd like it.

BRUCE: But don't you see, Edith—the attention should have been paid to *me,* not to *you.*

EDITH: He could hardly bring you flowers, Bruce.

BRUCE (*relenting*): Well, I won't make a mountain out of a molehill. I'll wait. I'll give him a chance.

EDITH: Exactly.

BRUCE: But if he comes here again, or takes any step to persuade you to have anything to do with his society or whatever it is, I'll know how to act.

EDITH: I hope you know, Bruce, *I* shouldn't care if I never saw him again.

BRUCE: *And why not?* Because he's my friend, I suppose? You look down on him just because he's a hard worker—not a wasp-waisted dandy like Cecil Reeve! Perhaps you prefer Cecil Reeve?

EDITH: Oh, much!

BRUCE: Let's hear your reasons.

EDITH: Well, Cecil Reeve is a real person. I know where I am when I'm talking with him. We're on the same platform.

BRUCE: The same platform?

EDITH: When I talk with Raggett I feel as if he'd arrived at Victoria Station and I'd gone to meet him at Charing Cross.

BRUCE: Edith, dear, I feel the need of air. I think I'll go for a stroll.

EDITH: Oh, Bruce!

BRUCE: Just a stroll. I may look in at the club. You don't understand, Edith. A man feels cramped in a tiny little flat like this.

EDITH: I *quite* understand.

BRUCE: I shan't be long. Try, Edith, and make up your mind to give up Raggett's society altogether.

EDITH: Yes, dear.

BRUCE (*at the door*): You don't mind making this sacrifice?

EDITH: Not in the least, dear. I really prefer it.

BRUCE (*suddenly*): Oh, Edith, dear—your *hair!* Your hair's coming down! (EDITH, *startled, touches her hair, finds it perfect.*) Your *hair*, Edith! Your hair! (*He goes out laughing.*)

CURTAIN

Scene Five

Afternoon. BRUCE *is seated in a chair, pencil and paper in hand, now and then jotting down notes.* EDITH *dashes in.*

EDITH: Bruce, dear, I wonder if you'd do me a very great favour.

BRUCE: That all depends, Edith.

EDITH: I've allowed Nurse to go out, and Bennett is busy, and I want to fly over just for a moment to see Hyacinth. She telephoned. I shan't be gone more than twenty minutes.

BRUCE (*annoyed at the interruption*): Of course, Edith, go. Do go. I don't want you. I'm very busy. (*He returns to his work.*)

EDITH: But, Bruce, dear, *would* you very much mind looking after Archie while I'm gone?

BRUCE: Archie?

EDITH: He'll be perfectly good. I'll give him his box of toys, and he'll sit in the corner, and you'll never notice he's there till I'm back again.

BRUCE: Of course. Of course. Surely I'm capable of looking after my own son. Do go.

EDITH: And if he asks for anything, just nod and smile and don't give it to him, and he'll be all right.

BRUCE: Oh, don't worry. And I say, Edith, just give him a hint I've got some rather important work to do, and he mustn't interrupt me by asking foolish questions.

EDITH: Of course, Bruce. I'm so glad you're not nervous at having to look after the child.

BRUCE: Nervous? *What* rot! I never heard such nonsense! I say, Edith—what's the doctor's address? In case he has a fit or something.

EDITH: Oh, Bruce! As if he'd *dream* of having a fit! Good gracious, don't make such a fuss!

BRUCE: I'm *not* making a fuss! It's *you* who are making a fuss! Fancy thinking it necessary to tell me not to give him what he asks for! As if I would! (*He returns to his work.* EDITH *brings in* ARCHIE, *a pretty little boy aged two, who gives his father a keen glance, then sits down in front of his box of toys.*)

EDITH: Good-bye, Archie, dear. I shan't be long. (*She kisses* ARCHIE *and goes out. There is a moment's silence.*)

ARCHIE (*holding out a card to* BRUCE): E for *ephalunt.* (BRUCE *frowns, waves his hand, continues his work.* ARCHIE *holds out another card.*) X for *swordfish.*

BRUCE: Don't talk, Archie.

ARCHIE: I've got my best suit on.

BRUCE (*absently*): Yes.

ARCHIE: What I was photographed in.

BRUCE: Don't talk, old chap. I want to work.

ARCHIE: This is my bear. It's the same bear.

BRUCE: The same bear as what?

ARCHIE: Just the same bear! This is a soldier. (*He puts a wooden soldier carefully in the box.*)

BRUCE: You want to have a talk, eh?

ARCHIE: Have you any sugar in your pockets?

BRUCE: Sugar in my pockets? Who put that in your head?

ARCHIE: Nobody didn't put it in my head. Don't you put sugar in your pockets?

BRUCE: Of course not! I'm not a parrot.

ARCHIE (*roaring with laughter*): You're not a parrot! Wouldn't it be fun if you was a parrot!

BRUCE: Don't be foolish, Archie.

ARCHIE: Do parrots keep sugar in their pockets?

BRUCE: Play with your soldiers, dear.

ARCHIE: Do parrots have pockets?

BRUCE: Don't be a nuisance, Archie.

ARCHIE: Why did you say parrots had sugar in their pockets?

BRUCE: I never said anything of the kind.

ARCHIE: Why do parrots have pockets?

BRUCE (*losing patience*): Do you think your mother will be long?

ARCHIE: Will Mother know about parrots and pockets?

BRUCE: You're talking nonsense, Archie. Your mother said you'd be good.

ARCHIE: Is it naughty to talk about parrots with pockets?

BRUCE: Yes.

ARCHIE: Then you're very naughty. You talk about parrots with pockets.

BRUCE: Will you stop talking about parrots if I get you some sugar?

ARCHIE: I'm a good boy. I'll stop talking about parrots if you get me some sugar.

BRUCE (*ringing the bell*): I really oughtn't to get you any. Your mother's sure to be angry.

ARCHIE: Do parrots have pockets?

BRUCE: You mustn't talk nonsense, Archie. (BENNETT *enters.*) Oh, Bennett, would you please give Archie six lumps of sugar.

BENNETT (*surprised, doubtful, amused*): Six lumps of sugar, sir?

BRUCE: Six. Do as I tell you.

BENNETT: Oh, yes, sir. Of course, sir. Come, Master Archie. (*She takes* ARCHIE*'s hand and they go out.* BRUCE *resumes his work. In a moment he hears the front door open and shut.*)

BRUCE (*calling*): Edith! (*A pause.*) Edith! (*Another pause.*) Oh, Edith!

(EDITH *appears at the door.*)

EDITH: Yes, Bruce?

BRUCE: Come here, Edith. I want to speak to you.

EDITH: Yes, dear.

BRUCE: Shut the door. (EDITH *comes in, shuts the door, stands waiting.*) Don't stand there. Come and sit down. (EDITH *sits down.*) Now, listen to me very seriously. I want to ask you a question.

EDITH: Yes?

BRUCE: How would you like for me to be making five thousand pounds a year—at least?

EDITH: Need you ask?

BRUCE: And all by my own talent!

EDITH (*trying not to look doubtful*): It would be jolly!

BRUCE: Jolly! I should think it would! I'll tell you what I've made up my mind to do.

EDITH: What?

BRUCE: I'm going to write a play.

EDITH (*trying to control her astonishment*): That's a very good idea.

BRUCE: *Such* a play! A really strong, powerful piece—all wit and cynicism and feeling and sentiment and that sort of rot. And it's going to be absolutely realistic. I don't mind telling you my model: Bernard Shaw. I like his style.

EDITH: It's the loveliest idea I ever heard of! And where do you plan to produce your play?

BRUCE: Oh, that depends. For some things I'd prefer His Majesty's, but I'm rather fond of the Haymarket too.

EDITH: The Haymarket!

BRUCE: But if the terms were right, I might give it to Charlie Hawtrey—or even Alexander if he offered me top royalties.

EDITH: Oh! Are you putting it up to auction?

BRUCE: Don't talk nonsense, Edith. I'll simply send a copy round to all the managers and see what they have to say. There's no reason why it shouldn't be quite as great a success as *The Merry Widow.*

EDITH: Oh, is it to be a comic opera?

BRUCE: Of course not! Didn't I tell you—it's to be a powerful play of real life.

EDITH: Tell me the plot.

BRUCE: I'll tell you *some* of the plot. At least, I'll tell you how it begins.

EDITH: Do go on!

BRUCE: Well, it begins in a rather unconventional way. The curtain goes up, and you find two servants—do you see—talking over their master and mistress. The maid—her name's Parker—is dusting the photographs, and she says to the manservant something about "The mistress does seem in a tantrum, doesn't she, Parker?" So he says—

EDITH: Are they both called Parker?

BRUCE: Yes—no—of course not! I forgot; it's the man who's called Parker. Well, they talk, and gradually let out a little of the plot. Then two friends of the hero come in, and—oh, I can't bother to tell you any more now. But isn't it rather a good idea?

EDITH: A capital idea! And so original! I do wish you'd be quick and do it, Bruce.

BRUCE: I *am* being quick. But you mustn't be in too great a hurry.

EDITH: Will it be ready in time for the season?

BRUCE: What! In a fortnight! How could they be ready to produce it in a fortnight? It won't be long; that I can promise you. I'm a quick worker…. And you mustn't be depressed, Edith, dear, if I get a little slating from some of the critics. You can't expect them all to appreciate a new writer at once. But the critics won't matter at all if my play pleases the public, which I don't mind telling you it's sure to do. Because, you see, it'll have all the good points and none of the bad points of all the successful plays of the last six years. That's my dodge. That's how I do it.

EDITH: I see!

BRUCE: Won't it be a joke when the governor and the mater are there on the first night! They'll be frightfully pleased. You must try and prevent the mater swaggering too much, you know. She's such a dear, she's sure to be absurdly proud. And it'll be a bit of a score off the governor too. He never would've thought I could do it, would he? You must have a ripping new dress for the first night, Edith, old girl.

EDITH: I think I'll have Liberty satin—that new shade of blue. But I won't order it just yet. You haven't written the first scene, have you?

BRUCE: The first scene! Of course not! Plays aren't done like that. The chief thing about a play like this is to get a scenario.

EDITH: A scenario?

BRUCE: A skeleton of the play. That's what I'll send round to the managers. They can see at once what it's going to be like.

EDITH: Have you settled on a name?

BRUCE: As a matter of fact I *have* settled on a name. But don't you go giving it away. I'm calling it *Lover Pro Tem*.

EDITH (*considering*): *Lover Pro Tem*.

BRUCE: Good name, isn't it?

EDITH: A splendid name. But isn't it a tiny bit like—

BRUCE: How unsympathetic you are, Edith! You don't understand!

EDITH: Oh, Bruce, I *do* understand! I *am* sympathetic! And I'm sure you'll have a great success. What fun it'll be! Will you work at it this afternoon?

BRUCE: Oh, no—not *this* afternoon. I'm rather tired out *this* afternoon with thinking. Perhaps I'll go and look in at the club. (*He goes out, leaving* EDITH *smiling quizzically.*)

CURTAIN

Act Two

Scene One

Afternoon. BRUCE *is lying on the sofa, recovering from influenza. Now and then he sneezes and coughs.* EDITH *enters.*

EDITH: Oh, Bruce, darling! How are you, dear? I do hope you're feeling better. (*She sits down by his side.*)

BRUCE (*sighing*): Oh, no, Edith—I'm feeling much worse. You know the usual results of influenza: heart failure, nervous depression leading to suicide—

EDITH: But you're much better, dear! Dr. Braithwaite said it was wonderful how quickly you threw it off.

BRUCE: Yes, but only because I have a marvellous constitution. Otherwise I might easily have been dead by now…. Edith, dear, I wish you'd go and fetch me some cigarettes.

EDITH: Certainly, Bruce. (*She rises and goes to the door.*)

BRUCE (*fretfully*): What are you fidgeting about, Edith? *Can't* you keep still? It's not at all good for a convalescent to have a restless person around.

EDITH: Why, Bruce, I was only going to fetch—

BRUCE: I know you were, dear; but you should learn repose. *Repose!* First you go out all morning, and when you come home you go rushing about the room.

EDITH (*sitting down again*): *Well,* Bruce! You'll be surprised to hear that Hyacinth Verney and Cecil Reeve are engaged.

BRUCE: Engaged!

EDITH: They're to be married in the autumn.

BRUCE: I never heard anything so idiotic in all my life!

EDITH: Why, Bruce!

BRUCE: A wedding in the autumn! A beastly time! October mists. November fogs.

EDITH: I heard something else even more surprising. Lord Selsey's to be married to Mrs. Raymond.

BRUCE: Lord Selsey! A widower! I thought he pretended to be so fond of his first wife.

EDITH: He was, dear. But she died eighteen years ago.

BRUCE: Instead of telling me all this tittle-tattle, Edith, why don't you go and fetch me the cigarettes?

EDITH: Certainly, dear. (*She rises and goes out.*)

BRUCE (*calling*): Of course I don't want to make a slave of you, Edith. But after all, they're only in the next room. And I'm very weak, or I'd go myself.

EDITH (*returning with the cigarettes*): Of course, dear.

BRUCE: Who is this Mrs. Raymond?

EDITH: Oh, she's a very nice woman—a widow. Really quite suitable for Lord Selsey. It seems he took the most violent fancy to her at first sight.

BRUCE: Well, they didn't consult *me! What* a pity! Lord Selsey always seemed to me such an agreeable chap.

EDITH (*smiling*): Oh, I think he'll be all right.

BRUCE: You're always smiling, Edith. Particularly when I have something to annoy me.

EDITH: I believe I read somewhere that a wife should always have a bright smile if her husband seemed depressed.

BRUCE: Good heavens, how awful! It'd be like living with a Cheshire cat!… Now, look here, Edith. It's very important that I don't see too many people at a time. You must arrange the visitors carefully. Who's coming this afternoon?

EDITH: I don't know of anyone—except perhaps your mother, and Mr. Raggett.

BRUCE: Ah—well, I can't see them both at once.

EDITH: Why not?

BRUCE: *Why not!* What a question! Because I can't stand the fatigue—that's why not! In fact, I'm not sure I ought to see Raggett at all.

EDITH: Then don't! Just leave a message to say you're not strong enough.

BRUCE: But if I do that, won't he think it rather a shame, poor chap, to come all this way—it *is* a long way, mind you—and then see nobody?

EDITH: Well, *I* can see him.

BRUCE: Oh, *you* want to see him, do you? Alone?

EDITH: Don't be silly, Bruce. I'd much rather *not* see him.

BRUCE: Indeed—*and why not?* I really believe you look down on him because he's my friend.

EDITH: Not a bit, dear. Not a bit.... But Raggett won't be angry. You can say you had a relapse or something and aren't well enough to see him.

BRUCE: Nothing of the sort! It'll be a splendid change to have a little intellectual talk with a man of the world. I've had all too much women's talk lately. I'm sick of it.... Ring the bell, Edith.

EDITH: Of course, Bruce, but what for? Is it anything I can do?

BRUCE: I want Bennett to pass me my tonic.

EDITH (*laughing*): Really, Bruce, it's at your elbow!

BRUCE (*mournfully, looking in the glass*): I suppose I've changed a good deal since my illness.

EDITH: You don't look at all bad, dear.

BRUCE: But sometimes, just as people are recovering, they suddenly have a frightful relapse. Braithwaite told me I'd have to be careful for some time.

EDITH: How long do you suppose he meant?

BRUCE: Oh, five or six years, I suppose. It's the heart. That's what's so risky in influenza.

EDITH: But he said your heart was all right!

BRUCE: Ah, so he *thinks*. Doctors don't know everything. Or perhaps it's what he *says;* it'd never do to tell a heart patient he was in danger. He might die on the spot from the shock.

EDITH: But, Bruce, dear, would he have taken me aside and told me you were perfectly well, and said he wouldn't come to see you again, if you were really in a dangerous state?

BRUCE: Very possibly. I don't know that I've so very much confidence in Braithwaite. When he seemed so sure of my recovery, I suggested he have a consultation.

EDITH: And what did he say?

BRUCE: He didn't see it! He refused!... Just go and get the cards, Edith—the cards left during my illness. I must write and thank everyone for their kindness.

EDITH: But there *are* no cards, dear.

BRUCE: *No cards!*

EDITH: You see, people who knew you were ill inquired by telephone.

BRUCE: So that's it! "Laugh, and the world laughs with you; weep, and you weep alone!" Get out of the running, and you're forgotten. And I'm a fairly popular man too. Yet I might have died like a dog in this wretched little flat, and not had a card.

EDITH: How about your play, Bruce? Couldn't you work at it this afternoon?

BRUCE: Oh, no—not just now. I'm not in the mood. You don't understand, Edith. The artist must work when the inspiration seizes him.

EDITH: Of course I know all that, Bruce. But it's been six months since you had the inspiration.

BRUCE: Besides, the trend of public taste gets worse and worse. Good heavens, I can't write down to the level of the vulgar public!

EDITH: But can you write at all?

BRUCE: Certainly! Certainly I can! But I need encouragement. *My* kind of talent, Edith, is like a flower—are you listening?—a flower that needs watering and tending. Appreciation—that's what *I* need.... Besides, *I'm* a businessman, and unless I have a proper contract with one of the managers—a regular agreement about my work being produced at a certain time—and, mind you, with a cast that *I* select—I just shan't do it at all.

EDITH: Have you taken any steps?

BRUCE: Of course I've taken steps—at least I've taken *stalls* at most of the theatres. There isn't a play going on at this moment that isn't full of faults—faults of the most blatant kind—mistakes that I myself would never have made. To begin with, take Shakespeare.

EDITH: Shakespeare?

BRUCE: Take a play like *The Merchant of Venice*. My dear girl, it's only the glamour of the name, believe me! It's a wretched play—improbable, badly constructed, full of padding. Good gracious! Do you suppose if *I'd* written that play and sent it to Tree, he'd have put it on?

EDITH: I can't suppose it, Bruce.

BRUCE: It doesn't make sense, Edith! Who ever heard of a case being conducted in any court of law as that is? Do you suppose all kinds of people are allowed to stand up and talk any nonsense that comes into their head—in blank verse too? Do you think if someone brought an action against me and you wanted to win it—do you think you and Bennett could calmly walk off to the law courts disguised as a barrister and his clerk and get me off? Do you suppose they'd even let you in?

EDITH: But this is poetry, Bruce, and years and years ago, in Elizabeth's time.

BRUCE: Then take a play like *The Merry Widow*. Do you suppose I couldn't do something better than that?... Look here, Edith, what's the point? Why are you so anxious I should write this play?

EDITH: Well, first of all, because I think it would amuse you.

BRUCE: Amuse me, indeed!

EDITH: And then far more because—Bruce, do you remember assuring me you were going to make five thousand pounds a year—at least?

BRUCE: Well, so I shall! So I shall! You must give a fellow time. Rome wasn't built in a day.

EDITH: Bruce, dear, if you're not going to work at your play, won't you just glance at the accounts?

BRUCE: You know perfectly well, Edith, if there's one thing I hate more than another it's glancing at accounts. Besides, what earthly use is it?

EDITH: It would be of use if you'd kindly explain how we're going to pay them.

BRUCE: Why, of course we're going to pay them—gradually.

EDITH: But they're getting bigger—gradually!

BRUCE: Dear me, Edith, didn't we a year or two ago make a budget? Didn't we write down exactly how much every single item of our expenditure would be?

EDITH: Yes, we did. But—

BRUCE: Well, good heavens, what more do you want?

EDITH: You made frightful mistakes in the budget, Bruce.

BRUCE: I remember I left a margin for unexpected calls.

EDITH: But you left out clothes altogether.

BRUCE: Oh, did I?

EDITH: And the margin went in a week—the first week of your holiday. You never counted holidays in the budget.

BRUCE: Oh, didn't I?

EDITH: You see, Bruce, we simply haven't enough for our expenses.

BRUCE: Then what's the use of looking at the accounts?

EDITH: To see where we are. What do you do when you receive a bill?

BRUCE: I throw it in the fire. I don't believe in keeping heaps of useless papers.

EDITH: But, Bruce, you really oughtn't to be in debt. All I want you to do is go through the bills with me to see how much we owe, how much we can pay, and how we can manage.

BRUCE: Oh, if *that's* all you want, of course we'll do it. But not this afternoon.

EDITH: Why not? You have nothing to do!

BRUCE: I know it's rather hard for you, dear girl, being married to a poor old man like me. But you know you *would* do it, and you mustn't reproach me now.

EDITH (*laughing*): We're not a bit too poor to have a very pleasant time, Bruce, if only you weren't so—

BRUCE: Go on—say it! You want to make out I'm extravagant. I *have* large ideas, I admit. It's difficult for me to be petty about trifles.

EDITH: Oh, Bruce, I'm not complaining about your large ideas. But you hardly ever give me a farthing. You expect me to do marvels on next to nothing.

BRUCE: All right, then—I'll give up smoking. I'll give up golfing. I'll give up all the little things that make life tolerable for a hard-working man.

EDITH: Not at all, dear! There's really only one luxury—if you won't think me unkind—only one luxury you might try to give up.

BRUCE: And what is that?

EDITH: Well, dear, couldn't you manage not to be *ill* quite so often? Whenever you're bored you have a consultation. The doctors always say you're quite all right. But it does rather—well, run up. Now, don't be angry with me.

BRUCE: Good God, Edith! If I didn't take it in time, you might be left a young widow, alone in the world, with Archie. Penny-wise and pound-foolish to neglect the health of the breadwinner! Do you reproach me because the doctor said I wasn't dangerously ill at the time?

EDITH: Of course not. I'm only too thankful.

BRUCE: Look here, Edith. I'll tell you what you can do. You're awfully good to worry about the bills; but I suggest you just run through them with my mother. She can advise you if you *have* gone into debt. She knows perfectly well it's not the sort of thing *I* can stand. And of course if she offers a little help— Well! She *is* my mother. I wouldn't hurt her feelings by refusing for anything in the world.

EDITH: But, Bruce, I'd much rather—

BRUCE: Oh, stop, Edith! Stop! I'm sorry to have to say it, but you're fast becoming a fussy old fidget.... And of course the whole thing about the accounts *must* have arisen from *your* want of management. But I won't reproach you, dear; I believe you mean well. (*Suddenly*) Good heavens, one of my headaches is coming on! I hope I'm not having another attack! (*He looks in the glass.*) I'm rather an odd colour, don't you think? (*A bell rings.*) What's that ring?

EDITH: It must be your mother.

BRUCE: Oh, dear! Oh, dear! (*He leans back on the sofa in a feeble attitude.*) Would you pull down the blinds, Edith, and put that vase of roses here on the table?

(EDITH *lowers the blinds and moves the roses as* BENNETT *shows in* MRS. OTTLEY. *She is a sweet woman, smartly dressed, with a charming smile and a good sense of humour.* BENNETT *goes out.*)

MRS. OTTLEY (*brightly*): Well! And how is the interesting invalid? Dear boy, how perfectly splendid you look!

BRUCE (*smiling faintly, speaking in a low voice*): Oh, hush, Mother! Do sit down and be quiet. Yes, I'm much better. But I'm still very, very weak.

MRS. OTTLEY: Dear, dear! (*To* EDITH) And what did the doctor say?

EDITH: He won't be coming any more.

MRS. OTTLEY (*to* BRUCE): Isn't he afraid you'll be rushing off to the office too soon? Oh, well—Edith will see that you take care of yourself. Where's little Archie?

EDITH: I'm afraid Archie's out.

MRS. OTTLEY (*to* EDITH): Oh, he *is* the sweetest darling! I see very little likeness to Bruce *or* his father. I think he takes after *my* family—with a great look of *you*, Edith.... Bruce, dear, what do you intend the boy to be when he grows up? Will you make him a useful member of society—or a Foreign Office clerk?

BRUCE: I intend my son—I intend my son— A little tonic, please, Edith. (EDITH *hands* BRUCE *the tonic.*) I intend my son to be a man of the world.

MRS. OTTLEY (*to* EDITH): Does he seem to show any particular bent?

EDITH: Well, he's very fond of soldiers.

MRS. OTTLEY: Soldiers!

EDITH: I don't mean he wants to *be* a soldier. But he likes playing with them. It's as much as I can do to keep him from *eating* them!

MRS. OTTLEY: The angel!

BRUCE: You must be careful about that, Edith. I understand red paint is poisonous.

EDITH: But he's just as fond of animals. (*To* MRS. OTTLEY) That Noah's ark you gave him is his greatest pleasure. He's always putting the animals in and taking them out.

MRS. OTTLEY: Oh, the clever child! You'd hardly believe it, Edith, but Bruce was like that when he was a little boy.

BRUCE: Oh, Mother, do shut up!

MRS. OTTLEY: You'd hardly think so now perhaps, but the things that child used to say!

BRUCE (*trying to change the subject*): Have you seen the new play at His Majesty's?

MRS. OTTLEY: Bruce, dear, are you eating well? Do try some of these almonds and raisins. (*To* EDITH) I always get my almonds and raisins at Harrods.

EDITH: They're the best almonds and raisins in the world.

(*A bell rings.*)

BRUCE (*sighing*): That's how it goes on all day long. People never cease calling. It's an infernal nuisance.

MRS. OTTLEY: Well, dear, it's nice to know you're not neglected.

EDITH: It's Mr. Raggett. I heard his voice. Will you see him, dear?

BRUCE: Take him in the other room, Edith, and when Mother goes he can come in here.

MRS. OTTLEY: I'm going now. You mustn't have a crowd. But really, Bruce, you're better than you think.

BRUCE (*sighing*): Well, I'm glad you think so.

MRS. OTTLEY: Your father wanted to know when you'd be going back to the office.

BRUCE: That all depends. I may be strong enough in a week or two, but I promised Braithwaite not to be rash…. Well, good-bye, Mother—if you *must* go.

MRS. OTTLEY (*kissing* BRUCE): Good-bye, my dear boy. Now, do be careful not to catch cold this treacherous spring weather. (*To* EDITH) What an angel Bruce is! So patient and brave! (*Confidentially, to* EDITH) Perfectly well, of course. He *has* been for a week. (*Shaking her head*) The image of his father! If I were you, Edith, *I'd* be ill too; it's the only way to get Bruce out…. Is he ever tiresome?

EDITH (*a bit too quickly*): Oh, no. Bruce is never tiresome.

MRS. OTTLEY (*sympathetically, pressing* EDITH*'s hand*): Darling! I *know* what it is. Mr. Ottley's been *most* trying lately. Do you suppose I've had a single instant to order a new bonnet?… His father thinks Bruce is a little bit selfish.

EDITH: Perhaps he's a little bit *spoilt.*

MRS. OTTLEY: Dear girl, may I give you a slight hint? Never contradict. Never oppose. Agree with him, and then he'll change his mind. Or if he doesn't, say you'll do as he wishes, and then act as your own judgement dictates. He'll never find out.

EDITH: May I go back with you a little, my dear?

MRS. OTTLEY: Oh, do! I'm going to Harrods, of course. I'm always going to Harrods. As Bruce has a friend, he'll let you leave. (*To* BRUCE) Good-bye, my dear. Good-bye!

EDITH (*kissing* BRUCE): Good-bye, Bruce, darling. I shan't be long.

BRUCE (*sighing*): Ah, Edith, suppose you'd married a chap

like Cecil Reeve—rolling in gold! Are he and Hyacinth happy, do you think?

EDITH: They seem *very* happy.

BRUCE: We're lunching there on Sunday, aren't we? Don't forget to order me a buttonhole, Edith.

EDITH: I shan't forget.

MRS. OTTLEY (*at the door*): It's not *next* Sunday, Bruce. *Next* Sunday you're lunching with *us*. You'll be sure to come, won't you?

BRUCE: Oh—ah—yes, Mother. Yes—*if* I'm well enough. But now will you please call in Raggett?

(MRS. OTTLEY *and* EDITH *go out, leaving* BRUCE *sighing on the sofa.*)

CURTAIN

Scene Two

Evening. EDITH *is seated on the sofa knitting;* BRUCE *is seated in a chair reading a book.*

BRUCE (*putting down his book*): Edith, dear.

EDITH: Yes, Bruce?

BRUCE: You know how strongly I disapprove of the modern fashion of husbands and wives each going their own way.

EDITH: Where are you thinking of going, dear?

BRUCE: Who said I was thinking of going anywhere?

EDITH: It's obvious, or you wouldn't have begun like that.

BRUCE: What did you think I was going to say next?

EDITH (*smiling*): You were going to say, after that sentence about "you know how strongly I disapprove"—you were going to say something like, "But of course there are exceptions to every rule, and in this particular instance I really think I'd better—"

BRUCE: Odd. Very odd you should get it into your head that I should have any idea of leaving you. Is that why you're laughing?

EDITH: Am I laughing? I thought I was only smiling.

BRUCE: I don't think it's a kind thing to smile at the idea of my going away. Well, I'm sorry to disappoint you, Edith—very sorry indeed. But as a matter of fact, I have no intention whatever of leaving you—except perhaps for a few hours at a time. Of course, if you wish, I might arrange to make it longer. Or even to remain away altogether if you prefer.

EDITH: Oh, Bruce, don't talk such nonsense! You know I wish nothing of the kind. What's this about a few hours at a time?

BRUCE: Naturally—naturally, when one has an invitation like this—oh, I admit it's a compliment—one doesn't want to decline without thinking it over. Think how absurd I'd appear to a man

like that, telling him my wife can't possibly spare me for a couple
of hours two or three times a week!

EDITH: Who is this mysterious man who wants you for a couple
of hours two or three times a week?

BRUCE: My dear, it can't be done without it. And though of
course it's rather a nuisance, I daresay in a way it won't be bad
fun. You'll help me, dear, and I'll arrange for you to see the
performance. Yes—you've guessed it: I've been asked to play in
some amateur theatricals being got up by Mitchell at the Foreign
Office in aid of the Society for the Suppression of Numismatics
or something. I can't think why he chose me, of all people!

EDITH: I wonder.

BRUCE: I don't see anything to wonder at. Perhaps he thought
I'd do it well. Perhaps he saw I had talent. He may have observed
I was threatened with intelligence! And of course they want a
fellow of decent appearance.

EDITH: Of course they do.

BRUCE: It would be absurd for the heroine of the play to be
madly in love with a chap who turned up looking like God knows
what! Not that I mean for a moment to imply that I'm particularly
good-looking, Edith. But—well, naturally, it's always an advantage
in playing the part of a leading man not to be quite bald and to
go in decently at the waist and to— Fancy, Miss Wrenner didn't
know I was a married man!

EDITH: Miss Wrenner! Who's Miss Wrenner?

BRUCE: Why, she— Don't you know who Miss Wrenner is?

EDITH: No!

BRUCE: Miss Wrenner's that girl who—a friend of the Mitchells. *You* know.

EDITH: I *don't* know. Miss Wrenner's quite new to me. So are
the Mitchells. What's she like?

BRUCE: *Like!* You ask me what she's *like!*

EDITH: Yes—what's Miss Wrenner like?

BRUCE: Why, she isn't *like* anything! She's just Miss Wrenner—
the well-known Miss Wrenner, the celebrated amateur actress.

EDITH: Is Miss Wrenner pretty?

BRUCE: Pretty? How do you mean?

EDITH: What colour is her hair?

BRUCE: Well, I—I—I didn't really notice.

EDITH: Is she dark or fair? You *must* know, Bruce.

BRUCE: Well, I should say she's a little darker than you. But I'm not quite certain…. Just fancy her not thinking I was married!

EDITH: Did you tell her?

BRUCE: Tell her! Of course I didn't tell her! Do you suppose a girl like Miss Wrenner's got nothing to do but collect marriage certificates?

EDITH: Then you *didn't* tell her.

BRUCE: Oh, yes, I did. Why should I palm myself off as a care-free bachelor when I'm nothing of the sort?

EDITH: When did you tell her, Bruce?

BRUCE: I haven't told her yet—at least, not personally. What happened was this: Mitchell said to me: "Miss Wrenner will be surprised to hear you're a married man."

EDITH: Where did all this happen?

BRUCE: At the Foreign Office. Where else do I ever see Mitchell?

EDITH: Then does Miss Wrenner come to the Foreign Office?

BRUCE: *Miss Wrenner at the Foreign Office!* You must be wool-gathering, Edith! Women aren't allowed at the Foreign Office!

EDITH: Well, then, where *did* you meet Miss Wrenner?

BRUCE: Why do you ask?

EDITH: Simply because I want to know.

BRUCE: Oh, good heavens! What does it matter *where* I met Miss Wrenner?

EDITH: You're right, Bruce. It doesn't really matter a bit.

BRUCE: I suppose I'll meet Miss Wrenner at the first rehearsal next week—at the Mitchells'.

EDITH: Was it there you met her before?

BRUCE: How *could* it be? I've never been to the Mitchells'.

EDITH: As a matter of fact, you've never met Miss Wrenner.

BRUCE: Did I say I had? What I intended to say was, not that I had met Miss Wrenner, but that *Mitchell* said Miss Wrenner would be surprised to hear I was married.

EDITH: Funny he should say that—curious it should occur to him to picture Miss Wrenner's astonishment at the marriage of a man she'd never met.

BRUCE: No, no, no, Edith! You've got the whole thing wrong. He—Mitchell—mentioned to me the names of the people who were going to be asked to act, and among them Miss Wrenner's name cropped up. I *think* he said Miss Wrenner was going to be asked to play the heroine if they could get her. (*Suddenly*) No—I'm wrong. He said *she* had *asked* to play the heroine, and they meant to get out of it if they could. So, *then, I* said, wouldn't she be surprised at having to play the principal part with a married man.

EDITH: So *you* said it, not Mitchell. Are *you* playing the hero?

BRUCE: Good gracious, no! Is it likely that Mitchell, who's mad on acting and is getting up the whole thing himself, would let *me* play the principal part? Is it human nature? I never said Mitchell wasn't human.

EDITH: What *is* your part, dear?

BRUCE: They're sending it to me tomorrow. It's not a big part, but Mitchell says there's a lot to be got out of it by a good actor. Sometimes one of these comparatively small parts, when really well played, can steal the show.

EDITH: What sort of part is it?

BRUCE: Oh, no particular *sort*. I don't come on until the second act. As I told you, one of the chief points is to have a good appearance—look a gentleman; that sort of thing.

EDITH: Well?

BRUCE: I come on in the second act dressed as a mandarin.

EDITH: A mandarin! Then you play the part of a Chinaman?

BRUCE: Not exactly. In the second act there's a ball for the hero's coming of age, and I have to be a mandarin.

EDITH: Is the ball given at the Chinese Embassy?

BRUCE: No—at the hero's country house. Didn't I tell you—it's a fancy ball!

EDITH: Oh, I *see!* Then I shouldn't have thought it would matter so very much whether you're good-looking or not. And Miss Wrenner—how will *she* be dressed at the fancy ball?

BRUCE: Miss Wrenner? Oh! Didn't I tell you? Miss Wrenner's not playing. She's not playing! They've found someone else to take her place.

(EDITH *shakes her head in bewilderment.*)

CURTAIN

Scene Three

Morning. BRUCE *and* EDITH *are seated at the breakfast table.* BRUCE *is reading a newspaper;* EDITH *is reading a letter.*

EDITH (*putting aside her letter*): Oh, Bruce, dear, I've just had a letter. Hyacinth wants me to go out with her this afternoon. It's the day you rehearse, isn't it?

BRUCE (*putting down his newspaper*): It's a curious thing, Edith—you can't get Cook to make a hot omelette.

EDITH: It *was* a hot omelette, Bruce, three-quarters of an hour ago. Shall I order another?

BRUCE: Oh, no—not for me. I haven't the time. You have rather a way, Edith, of keeping me talking. You seem to think I've nothing else to do.... Oh, by the way—I shouldn't go out with Hyacinth today if I were you.

EDITH: Why not, Bruce?

BRUCE: Well, I may want you.

EDITH: Then aren't you going to the Mitchells'?

BRUCE: The Mitchells'! I'm certainly *not* going to the Mitchells'!

EDITH: But, Bruce—

BRUCE: How you can expect me to go to the Mitchells' is more than I can understand! Have you no pride, Edith?

EDITH: Why, Bruce! Has anything happened? What have the Mitchells done?

BRUCE: *Done!* What have they *done!* How do you think I've been treated by those Mitchells—after slaving night and day at their infernal theatricals? I *have* slaved, haven't I, Edith?

EDITH: Indeed you have, dear.

BRUCE: Well, you know the last rehearsal? I got on particularly well. I threw a good deal of emotion and also a tinge of irony into my speech to Miss Vavasour. A lot hinges on that speech, and it isn't everyone who could make the most of it.... Well, yesterday at the office I happened to mention to Mitchell how much I'd done for his play, and how much time I'd given up towards making the thing a success—when what do you think he turned and said?

EDITH: I can't think!

BRUCE: Oh, he *is* a brute! "Ottley, old chap, we've altered our plans a little, and I really don't think we need trouble you after all. The fact is, we've decided to cut out the fancy ball altogether."

EDITH: Altogether!

BRUCE: And then people talk of gratitude!

EDITH: Oh, Bruce, dear, it *does* seem a pity!

BRUCE: A *pity!* Is that all you have to say? It's an *outrage*—that's what it is—a slight on *me!* It isn't treating *me* with proper deference.… Of course I don't care personally; it's the principle of the thing that counts. For my own sake I'm only too pleased; it's for *their* sake I'm sorry. The whole thing is bound to be a failure now. The fancy ball in the second act, and especially my little scene with Miss Vavasour, was the point of the play.

EDITH: Then why is he cutting out the fancy ball?

BRUCE: He says they can't get enough people. Says they won't buy fancy dresses just to make one in a crowd. Says the fancy ball for the hero's coming of age would've consisted of one mandarin, one Queen of the Night, and a chap in a powdered wig.

EDITH: Well, I *am* sorry! Still, couldn't you say your part just the same in ordinary dress?

BRUCE: Oh, Edith, you forget the lines! "Ah, Miss Vavasour, how charming you look—a true Queen of the Night! May a humble mandarin petition for a dance?" How could I say those lines if we weren't in fancy dress?

EDITH: Still, if the whole plot hinges on your scene—

BRUCE: All I know is, out it goes—and out *I* go. Of course, they're making a terrible mistake. But that's Mitchell's business, not mine. It's no deprivation to *me*. What possible gratification could it be for a man like me—a man of the world—to paint my face and put on a ridiculous dress and make a general fool of myself, just to help Mitchell's rotten performance go off all right!

EDITH: Still, it might have amused you. In any case, I'm sorry.

BRUCE: *I'm* sorry too—sorry for *them*. But if you really want to know the root of the matter, Edith, it's jealousy! Yes, jealousy! It's odd, when people get keen on this sort of thing, how vain they become. Perfectly childish! The plain truth is, old Mitchell doesn't want me to make a hit. Rather thick, isn't it, when you remember the hours I've worked for that man!

EDITH: What did you say to him, Bruce, when he first told you?

BRUCE: I said nothing. I took it all as a man of the world. I merely said, "Well, upon my word, Mitchell, this *is* pretty rough," or something like that. I didn't show I was hurt in any way. I *did* say it was just like his beastly ingratitude—

EDITH: Oh! Was he angry?

BRUCE: He was furious.

EDITH: Then you've had a quarrel with Mitchell.

BRUCE: Not a quarrel, Edith, because *I* won't quarrel. I merely rubbed in his ingratitude. "Well," he said, "let's hope if you're no longer wasting your valuable life on my theatricals you'll now be able to arrive at the office in fairly decent time."

EDITH: Well, my dear, you must tell me all about it this afternoon.

BRUCE: But, Edith, that wasn't all! Mitchell actually said he didn't think I had the smallest talent for the stage! He said I made too much of my part—overacted—exaggerated! The fact is, Mitchell's a conceited ass. He knows no more about acting than that chair, and he thinks he knows everything.

EDITH: It's fortunate you hadn't ordered your costume.

BRUCE: Indeed. As I told him, the whole thing might have cost me a tremendous lot—far more than I could afford. And all for nothing! But he said the costumer would probably take it back; and if he wouldn't, I could send the costume to him—Mitchell—*and* the bill. As if I'd *dream* of letting *him* pay for it! I told him at once there could be no question of such a thing.

EDITH: Well, there won't be, as you haven't ordered it.

BRUCE: Now, Edith, let me beg you not to argue. Isn't it bad enough that I'm slighted by my so-called friends, and treated with the basest ingratitude, without being argued with in my own home?

EDITH: I didn't know I was arguing. But you mustn't worry about this, dear. If they found they didn't really *need* a mandarin—I mean, the fancy-ball scene wasn't necessary—perhaps from *their* point of view they were right to cut it out. Don't have a lasting feud with Mitchell. Isn't he rather an important friend for you—at the office?

BRUCE: Edith, Mitchell will never again set foot under my roof. He'll never darken these doors again!

EDITH: I wonder why, when people are angry, they talk about roofs and doors. If you were *pleased* with Mitchell again, you wouldn't *ask* him to set foot under your roof; you wouldn't *ask* him to darken your door. Anyhow, he won't feel it so very much—he's never been here yet.

BRUCE: But Mrs. Mitchell was going to call. You'll be out to her now, remember.

EDITH: I can safely promise, Bruce, never to receive Mrs. Mitchell.

BRUCE (*suddenly, looking at the clock*): Good heavens! Do you know what time it is? (*Starting up*) I told you so! I told you so! (*At the door*) Edith, dear, you've made me late again at the office! (*He rushes out.*)

CURTAIN

Scene Four

Early evening. EDITH *is seated on the sofa knitting.* BRUCE *enters, just back from his office.*

EDITH: Oh, hello, Bruce.

BRUCE: Hallo, Edith, dear. (*He kisses* EDITH *perfunctorily on the cheek.*)

EDITH: I hope you're feeling better tonight, Bruce. How's your temperature?

BRUCE: Oh, *I* don't know. I can't worry about *that*. A rather nice thing happened today—in fact *very* nice.

EDITH: Oh, really? Do tell me!

BRUCE: Edith, however badly a chap behaves—still, when he's truly sorry, when he climbs down and begs your pardon and positively crawls at your feet, you can't hold out.

EDITH: Of course not.

BRUCE: And when you've known a fellow a good many years, and he's always been fairly decent to you except in the one instance, and he's in real difficulty—oh, hang it! I'm glad to do what I can.

EDITH (*smiling*): Do I gather there's been a touching scene between you and Mitchell at the office?

BRUCE: May I ask if you're laughing?

EDITH: Of course not, Bruce. I'm smiling with pleasure, hoping you've made it up.

BRUCE: Well, yes—it may be weak of me, but I couldn't see the poor fellow's scheme absolutely *ruined* without lending a helping hand. *I've* got my share of proper pride, as you well know, Edith. But after all, one has a heart.

EDITH: What did Mitchell do?

BRUCE: Do! Do! He apologized—that's what he did! He begged me to act with them again. He said the piece was nothing without me. So of course I forgave him. And he was jolly grateful, I can tell you!

EDITH: Is it the same part?

BRUCE: Of course not! The fancy ball in the second act has been cut out, so of course they don't want a mandarin. But Frank Luscombe has chucked his part, and they've asked me to take it.

EDITH: Is it as long as the other part?

BRUCE: Longer! I appear twice! Mind you, in a way it's not *quite* as important a part as the other would've been. But the play wouldn't hold together without it. And as Mitchell said, Frank Luscombe thought himself too grand to play a footman. He was grumbling all the time and at last gave it up. Then it occurred to Mitchell that perhaps *I'd* help him out. It *is* a bit of a triumph, isn't it, Edith?

EDITH: A great triumph. Then you'll be going back to rehearsals again?

BRUCE: Of course I will; they begin tomorrow. And Mitchell thinks I'll make the hit of the evening. He saw during rehearsals what tremendous talent I have. But it isn't merely talent. What they all noticed was my personal magnetism.... Fancy! A man like Mitchell comes cringing to *me* after all that's passed between us! Mind you, Edith, it's a distinct score!

EDITH: It is indeed.... But, Bruce, dear, if you haven't got your part with you, you won't want to work at it tonight. I wonder, as you seem better, whether you'd feel up to listening while I tell you something about the accounts.

BRUCE: There you go! There you go! How like a woman! The very moment I'm feeling a bit cheered up you begin worrying me again.

EDITH: Dear Bruce, I'm not worrying you. You remember you said you weren't strong enough to go through the accounts, and suggested I show them to your mother. Well, I went today, and I only want to tell you what happened.

BRUCE: Jolly good of you. What did she say?

EDITH: She thought she could arrange it, but not without speaking to your father.

BRUCE: Well, that's all right, then!... The girl who plays Miss Vavasour is quite as good as any professional actress; she'd have made a fortune on the stage. She's a Miss Flummerfelt. If she weren't just a little bit inclined to be fat, she'd be wonderfully handsome. I have a little scene with her in the third act—not really a scene exactly, but I have to announce her. I open the door and say, "Miss Vavasour!" And then she rushes up to Lady Jenkins, who's sitting on the sofa, and tells her the bracelet has been found. And then I shut the door. But there's a great deal, you know, in the tone in which I announce her. Frank Luscombe, it seems, used to say the words without any expression at all.

EDITH: I see.... Your father was at home at the time, so your mother kindly said she'd go in to see him at once and try to get it settled, just to spare you the suspense of waiting for a letter. Wasn't that sweet of her!

BRUCE: Awfully.... In the second act, Lady Jenkins says to me, "Parker, has an emerald bracelet with a ruby head been found in any of the rooms?" And I have to say, "I will inquire, my lady." And then I move about the room, putting things in order. And then she says, "That will do, Parker; you can go."

EDITH: Splendid!... But do listen, Bruce. I waited, feeling frightfully uncomfortable, and I'm afraid there was a fearful row. But you know the way your mother has of going straight to the point.

BRUCE: Of course, there's one thing Mitchell asked me to do, but I was obliged to refuse. I can't shave off my moustache.

EDITH: Heavens! You aren't going to play the part of a footman wearing a moustache!

BRUCE: Mitchell doesn't know it yet, but I mean to. I can carry it off. *I* can carry off anything!

EDITH: Well, your mother came back and said your father had given an ultimatum.

BRUCE: Is *that* all he's given!

EDITH: He'll set the whole thing straight on one condition. He'll write and tell you. Your mother says you must agree at once, not argue, and then everything will be all right.

BRUCE: Oh, I *am* glad.... You should've seen how pleased Mitchell was when I said I'd do this for him. Oh—and Mrs. Mitchell is going to call on you.

EDITH: I suppose I'm to be at home to her now?

BRUCE: If you could manage it without being rude, Edith, I'd rather she only left a card. The Mansions look all right from outside, and they *are* in a decent neighbourhood, but the flat is so *very* small.

EDITH: Really, Bruce, you are absurd! Does Mitchell suppose you live in a palace?

BRUCE: Not a *palace,* exactly. But I expect I *have* rather given him an impression it's—well—all right.

EDITH: And so it is! If you think the flat unworthy to be seen by Mrs. Mitchell, why be on visiting terms with her at all?

BRUCE: But, Edith—you can't refuse the advances of a woman like that, the wife of a special friend. You've no idea how upset Mitchell was about our little quarrel the other day. He said he couldn't sleep at night thinking about it. And his wife, too, was fretting dreadfully. But now, of course, it's all right.

EDITH: I'm not so sure it's all right. Perhaps you'll quarrel again—over the moustache.

BRUCE: No, no, no! There won't be any more chopping and changing. After telling the whole company we've buried the hatchet and I'm taking Luscombe's part, he wouldn't dare disappoint them again. Old Mitchell will be too pleased to get me back to worry about a trifling moustache!

(BENNETT *enters.*)

BENNETT: If you please, ma'am, dinner is served.

EDITH: Oh, thank you, Bennett. (EDITH *and* BRUCE *rise.* BENNETT *goes out.*) Bruce, dear, do you mind writing to your mother tonight—just a line to thank her for being so kind? It was awfully nice of her, you know—she stuck up for you like anything. And she's spared you having a scene with your father.

BRUCE: Yes, Edith, you told me before. But I have to write an important letter tonight. I'll write to the mater tomorrow.

EDITH: Oh, Bruce!

BRUCE: My dear girl, business first, pleasure after. To write to one's mother is a pleasure.

EDITH: But, Bruce—

BRUCE: Look here, Edith—don't take any engagements for the next two or three weeks. I'll want you every evening for rehearsing. I mean to make a good job of this. *A good job!* And who knows? I just may give Miss Elsa Flummerfelt the surprise of her life! (*His voice trails off as they go out together.*)

CURTAIN

Scene Five

Morning. BRUCE *and* EDITH *are seated at the breakfast table.* BRUCE *is reading a newspaper;* EDITH *is pouring coffee.*

BRUCE (*from behind his newspaper*): Edith, dear.

EDITH: Yes, Bruce?

BRUCE (*putting down his newspaper*): I'm rather worried about Raggett.

EDITH: Raggett? *Are* you, dear!

BRUCE: The last time I met him, he asked me if I knew the difference between a sardine and a hedgehog. Of course I said no, thinking it was some riddle; but he only answered, "Then you *must* be a fool!"

EDITH (*smiling*): Is *that* all!

BRUCE: No, it's *not* all! It'll give you a shock—what I'm about to tell you. At the office—at the Foreign Office, mind—I received a letter from Raggett *written on a crumpet.*

EDITH: On a *what?*

BRUCE: On a crumpet. The letter was gummed on; the thing had a stamp, and was properly addressed to me, and it came through the post. And what do you think the postscript said?

EDITH: I can't think.

BRUCE: "Please excuse my writing to you on a crumpet, as I don't have a muffin." (EDITH *laughs.*) It's all very well for you to laugh, Edith, but it's really a sad thing. The poor chap is going off his head!

EDITH: He isn't really, Bruce. I can explain the whole thing.

BRUCE: *Explain?*

EDITH: The last time I saw Raggett—he called here the day you were rehearsing—he said he's given up being a Legitimist, and is trying if possible to develop a sense of humour.

BRUCE: A sense of *humour!*

EDITH: He hopes the story of the crumpet will please *me.*

BRUCE: Do you seriously mean he's trying to be funny on *your* account?

EDITH: That's the idea.

BRUCE: You admit openly, Edith, he has such a liking for you he's becoming a clown in the hope *you'll* find him *witty?*

EDITH: That's it. He's afraid he's a bore. He wishes to amuse me.

BRUCE: What right has he to wish anything of the kind? Haven't you got *me* if you wish to be amused?

EDITH: Oh, Bruce—

BRUCE: If I thought you were right—but, mind you, I don't; all women have their little vanities, and I believe it's a delusion of yours about Raggett. I think he's simply getting a little queer in the head.

EDITH: Bruce—

BRUCE: If I thought you were right, of course, I'd consider it an outrage. To write me a letter on a crumpet—*as a joke!* Joke, indeed! Men have been called out for less, Edith!... I'll take no notice of it this time. But if I have any more nonsense from Raggett, I'll demand an explanation: "My wife tells me your tone, which I consider greatly wanting in deference to *me,* is meant as homage to *her.*" (*Fiercely*) I'll say to Raggett, just like this, "What the—?"

EDITH: No, no, Bruce—you mustn't bully poor Raggett. Perhaps he wants to amuse us both.

BRUCE (*relenting*): Perhaps. Perhaps. But he's working the wrong way if he hopes to keep *my* good opinion.

EDITH: Instead of bothering about Raggett, I do wish you'd answer your father's letter, Bruce.

BRUCE: Oh, Edith! Surely I needn't answer it today!

EDITH: I think you should.

BRUCE: Well, what does he say?

EDITH: I've told you already, Bruce, but you wouldn't listen. On condition you're not late at the office or absent for any reason, either pleasure or illness, for the next two years, your father will pay the debt and help you start afresh.

BRUCE: But how can I be sure I shan't be ill? A man in *my* delicate state!

EDITH: Oh, assume that you won't. Try not to be. Surely it's worth it?

BRUCE: What a curious man the governor is! No other man would set such extraordinary conditions.... Look here, Edith—*you* can write *for* me and say I accept the arrangement, and I'm awfully grateful and all that. You'll know how to put it. It's a great nuisance, though, for I was thinking of giving up the whole of tomorrow to rehearsing—and chucking the office.

EDITH: Well, I'll write *for* you, Bruce—though you certainly ought to do it yourself. But I'll say you're going to see them. And you will—next Sunday, won't you?

BRUCE: Next Sunday would be rather awkward, Edith. I've— I've made a sort of vague engagement.

EDITH: I can't quite understand why rehearsals take so long now. Yesterday you said you had to begin at eleven and it wasn't over till half-past four. And yet you have only two or three words to say in the second act and one line in the third.

BRUCE: You don't understand, my dear. One has to be there the whole time so as to get into the spirit of the thing. Rehearsals sometimes take half the night—especially when you're getting near the end. You just stop for a minute or two for a little food, and then you start again. Yesterday, for instance, it was just like that.

EDITH: Where did you lunch?

BRUCE: Oh, I and one or two others looked in at the Carlton.

EDITH: And what are you doing tomorrow?

BRUCE (*hesitating*): Oh, tomorrow? Well, now, after this promise to the governor I shan't be able to get there till half-past four. I'd hoped to get there by twelve. And it's very awkward indeed, because Miss Flummerfelt asked me to take her to lunch, and I half promised.

EDITH: She asked you to take her alone?

BRUCE: Oh, in a thing like this you all become such pals you don't stop to think about chaperones. Besides, I meant to ask you to join us.

EDITH: Very sweet of you, I'm sure.

(BENNETT *enters bringing a letter on a salver.*)

BRUCE: Ah—here's the post. (*He takes the letter.*) Thank you, Bennett. (BENNETT *goes out.*)

EDITH: Who's your letter from?

BRUCE (*hesitating*): It *looks* something like Miss Flummerfelt.

EDITH: Miss Flummerfelt! (BRUCE *opens the letter and reads, then goes to the fire to throw it in.*) Oh, Bruce—do show me the letter!

BRUCE (*resisting*): Edith, dear—

EDITH: Bruce, *please!* (BRUCE *reluctantly hands* EDITH *the letter. She reads.*) "Dear Mr. Ottley, It's very kind of you to ask me to lunch tomorrow, but I'm already engaged, besides which I never go anywhere without my mother. Yours sincerely, Elsa Flummerfelt." (*Looking up*) Well, how very fortunate! Now you won't have the awkwardness of putting her off.

BRUCE (*a bit too quickly*): I assure you, Edith, I felt I ought—as a matter of decent civility to Mitchell—to ask her once. I suppose now you won't like my going to rehearsals.

EDITH: Oh, no! Not at all! Now I see what a nice girl Miss Flummerfelt must be!

BRUCE: I see nothing particularly nice about her.

EDITH: But she's wonderfully handsome, isn't she?

BRUCE: Handsome! She has a clumsy figure, drab hair, a colourless complexion. Not at all my type.

EDITH: You told me the other day she was an ideal blonde. But of course that was before she refused to lunch with you.

BRUCE: Edith, dear, I can assure you—

EDITH: How did you get on yesterday?

BRUCE: Oh, Edith, you can't think how much jealousy there is! When you rehearse with people day after day you begin to find out what they're really like. And Mitchell has a nasty temper. First of all, there was a scene over whether or not I should shave for the part of the footman. *He* said I ought; *I* said I wouldn't ruin my appearance just for the sake of a miserable little part like that. At last we compromised. I'm to wear something that gums down the moustache, so that you don't notice it.

EDITH: But you don't notice it much anyhow.

BRUCE: What do you mean by that?

EDITH: I don't mean anything. But I never heard of anybody's noticing it.

BRUCE: It can't have passed *un*noticed, because if it had, why should Mitchell ask me to shave?

EDITH: There's something in that, I must admit.

BRUCE: Well, I consented to Mitchell's suggestion, though I don't like it at all, and I daresay it'll spoil my appearance altogether.

EDITH: So you quarrelled with Mitchell again.

BRUCE: We had a few words.

EDITH: A few words?

BRUCE: I told Mitchell what I thought of him in no uncertain terms. I even went so far as to threaten to throw up my part. And then he said, "Well, all right, Ottley, if you don't like it you can give it up at any time." I said, "Who else could you get at the last minute to play a footman's part?" And he said, "Our footman!"

EDITH (*smiling*): That *would* be realism, wouldn't it?

BRUCE: So it was settled I was to stick to my part.

EDITH: It's with the woman who plays Lady Jenkins you have your longer scene, isn't it?

BRUCE: Mrs. Abbott, you mean.

EDITH: What is *she* like?

BRUCE: Oh, I don't think much of *her*. She's acted before and thinks she's quite as good as a professional. She's the most absurd snob you ever saw. She had the cheek to say I don't move about the room naturally, like a real footman. I told her I'd never been one. "Still," she said, "you might have *seen* one."

EDITH (*sympathetically*): You'll be glad when it's all over, won't you, dear?

BRUCE: The strain is telling on my health. But I've been better on the whole, don't you think?

EDITH: Oh, yes, Bruce. You've been much better. You have to be.

BRUCE: Of course—I have to be. Now, *please,* Edith—*please* don't make me late again at the office!

(*They go out together arm-in-arm.*)

CURTAIN

Tenterhooks

Tenterhooks, a comedy in two acts, is drawn from the novel *Tenterhooks,* by Ada Leverson, first published in London in 1912.

CHARACTERS

Edith Ottley

Archie Ottley

Bruce Ottley

Bennett

Vincent Wenham Vincy

Aylmer Ross

SCENES

Time: 1912

Place: London

The scene is set in the drawing room of the
Ottley flat in Linden Mansions, Cadogan Square

ACT ONE

Scene 1   Afternoon

Scene 2   Morning

Scene 3   Afternoon

ACT TWO

Scene 1   Evening

Scene 2   Morning

Scene 3   Afternoon

Scene 4   Early evening

Act One

Scene One

The drawing room of the Ottley flat in Linden Mansions, Cadogan Square, London. Afternoon. It is a comfortable, pleasant, informal room agreeably furnished. A fire is burning on the hearth.

At rise EDITH OTTLEY, *aged thirty-one, intelligent, charming, and very pretty, is at the telephone.*

EDITH: Hello…. Hello…. Oh!… Exchange, *why* are you ringing off? *Please* try again…. Do I want any number? Yes, of course I want any number, or why should I ring up?… I want 6375 Gerrard.

(ARCHIE OTTLEY *enters. He is a pretty little boy aged six.*)

ARCHIE: Mother, can I have your long buttonhook?

EDITH: No, Archie, you can't just now, dear…. Yes, I said 6375 Gerrard…. Gerrard!… Go away, Archie…. Oh, *don't* keep asking me if I've got them!… No, they *haven't* answered…. Are you 6375?… Oh—wrong number. Sorry…. 6375 Gerrard?… Are you there?… *Not* 6375 Gerrard?… Are you anyone else?… Ho, is it you, Vincy?… Darling Vincy, I want to tell you—

ARCHIE: Mother, can I have your long buttonhook?

EDITH: Certainly *not*, dear…. Oh, Vincy, that was Archie, asking for my long buttonhook…. Vincy, dear, I just wanted to tell you— (BRUCE OTTLEY, *aged thirty-three, tall, good-looking, and well built, enters.*) Oh, Vincy, here comes Bruce…. Yes…. Shall I ring you back?… What?… Why, yes, darling—of course we're here!… Yes…. Yes…. In fifteen minutes…. Of course!… Good-bye, my dear…. Good-bye. (*She hangs up.* ARCHIE *goes out.*) Oh, hello, Bruce, darling. I was just talking to Vincy. He's coming right over.

69

BRUCE: It's really rather wonderful, Edith, what that Sandow exerciser has done for me! You laughed at me at first, but I've improved marvellously.

EDITH: Have you, dear?

(BRUCE *walks about doing mild gymnastics, occasionally hitting himself on the left arm with the right fist.*)

BRUCE: Look at my muscle—look at it! And all in such a short time!

EDITH: Splendid!

BRUCE: Something I've just done I couldn't have done before. Of course I'm naturally a very powerful man, and only need a little—

EDITH: What have you done, dear?

BRUCE: Why, you know that great ridiculous old wooden chest your awful Aunt Matilda sent you for your birthday? Absurd present, *I* call it—mere lumber.

EDITH: Yes?

BRUCE: When it came I could barely push it from one side of the room to the other. Now I've lifted it from your room to the box room. Pretty good, isn't it?

EDITH: Yes, of course, Bruce, it's very good for you to do all these exercises…. Uh—you know, dear, don't you, I've had all the things taken out of the chest since you tried it before.

BRUCE: Things? What things?

EDITH: Only a silver tea service, and a couple of heavy salvers, and four sauceboats, and eight candlesticks, and a set of cutlery for twenty-four, and—

BRUCE (*eagerly, changing the subject*): Edith, dear, I have good news!

EDITH: Good news?

BRUCE: You know the Mitchells.

EDITH: Do *I* know the Mitchells! Mitchell, your hero at the Foreign Office, the man you're always offended with. At least I know the Mitchells *by name*.

BRUCE: Well, what do you think they've done?

EDITH: I can't think, Bruce.

BRUCE: They've asked us to dinner!

EDITH: *Have* they!

BRUCE: Mitchell said to me, just like this: "Ottley, old chap, are you doing anything on Sunday evening?"

(ARCHIE *reappears at the door.*)

ARCHIE: Mother, can I have your long buttonhook?

EDITH: Certainly *not*, dear.

BRUCE: "Ottley, old chap, are you and your wife doing anything on Sunday? If not, I do wish you'd waive ceremony and come and dine with us. Would Mrs. Ottley excuse a verbal invitation, do you think?" I said, "Well, Mitchell, as a matter of fact I don't believe we've got anything on. Yes, old boy, we'll be delighted." I accepted, you see. I accepted straight out. When you're treated in a friendly way, I always say why be unfriendly. And Mrs. Mitchell is a charming little woman. It seems she's been dying to know *you*.

EDITH: I wonder she's still alive, then, since you and Mitchell have known each other eight years, and I've not met her yet.

BRUCE: Well, you will now. They live in Hamilton Place.

EDITH: Oh, yes—Park Lane.

BRUCE: I told you he's doing very well, and his wife has private means.

ARCHIE (*beginning again*): Mother, can I have your long buttonhook?

EDITH: No, Archie, certainly *not*. You can't fasten laced boots with a buttonhook.... Well, that will be fun, Bruce.

BRUCE: What will you wear, Edith?

ARCHIE (*insistent*): Mother, do let me have your long buttonhook.

EDITH: Certainly *not*, Archie, dear. What a nuisance you are!... I think I'll wear my salmon-coloured dress with the mayonnaise-coloured sash.... No, you're not to have it, Archie!

ARCHIE: But, Mother—I've already got it!

EDITH: Archie!

BRUCE (*impatient*):Well, I leave him to you, my dear.

EDITH: Oh, Bruce!

(BRUCE *goes out.*)

ARCHIE (*sweetly*): Mother!

EDITH (*relenting*): What is it, dear?

ARCHIE: I had such a lovely dream last night.

EDITH: Did you, pet? How sweet of you!

ARCHIE: I dreamt I was in heaven.

EDITH: In heaven! Really! How delightful! Who was there?

ARCHIE: Oh, you were there, of course. And Father. *Such* a nice place!

EDITH: Was Vincy there?

ARCHIE: Oh, yes!

EDITH: Was Bennett there?

ARCHIE: Oh, yes!

EDITH: Was Miss Townsend there?

ARCHIE: Miss Townsend? Uh—no—Miss Townsend wasn't there.

EDITH: Miss Townsend wasn't there!

ARCHIE: Miss Townsend was in the night nursery—with Satan.

EDITH: Archie, darling! You mustn't speak of Miss Townsend that way. Miss Townsend is your governess!

(BRUCE *rushes in.*)

BRUCE: Will you please tell me, Edith, where your son Archie learns such vile language?

EDITH: Vile language!

BRUCE: He keeps on worrying me to take him to the Zoological Gardens to see the—well—you'll hear what he says.

EDITH: Archie, darling—

BRUCE: The child's a perfect nuisance. Who put it in his head to want to see that animal?

EDITH: What animal?

BRUCE: You must be firm with him, Edith. *Firm.* Good heavens! Am I master in my own house or am I not? (*Turning to* ARCHIE) Archie, old chap, tell your mother what it is you want to see.

ARCHIE: I want to see the damned chameleon.

EDITH: You want to see the *what?*

ARCHIE: I want Father to take me to the zoo—to see the damned chameleon.

EDITH: Archie, you can't go to the zoo this afternoon.

ARCHIE: I want to see the damned chameleon!

BRUCE (*to* EDITH): You hear?

EDITH: Archie, darling, who taught you this language?

ARCHIE: Miss Townsend.

EDITH: *Miss Townsend!*

BRUCE: There! It's dreadful, Edith. He's becoming a reckless liar. Fancy her *dreaming* of teaching him such things! If she did, of course, she must be mad, and you must send her away at once.

EDITH: Come, Archie—you know Miss Townsend never taught you to say that.

ARCHIE: Well, she didn't exactly *teach* me to say it. But she says it herself.

EDITH: She says it herself!

ARCHIE: She said the damned chameleon was lovely.

BRUCE (*to* EDITH): You hear?

ARCHIE: She didn't say I *ought* to see it. But I want to. Lots of other boys go to the zoo. Why shouldn't I?

BRUCE: Edith, you must speak to Miss Townsend about this. People have no right to talk to the boy about queer animals—and in such language!

EDITH: Bruce, dear—

BRUCE: I should've thought a girl like Miss Townsend, who has passed examinations in Germany, would've had more sense. And the daughter of a clergyman too!

EDITH (*laughing*): Bruce, dear, it's all right!

BRUCE (*staring*): All *right!*

EDITH: Miss Townsend told me some time ago she'd been to see *La Dame aux camélias.*

BRUCE: She'd been to see *what?*

EDITH: *La Dame aux camélias.* A play—from the novel by Dumas.

BRUCE: Dumas!

EDITH: But never mind, Archie, dear. I'll take you to the zoo, and we'll see lots of other animals. And please, darling, never, never use that expression again.

(BENNETT *enters.*)

BENNETT (*announcing*): Mr. Vincy!

(VINCENT WENHAM VINCY *enters. He is thirty-eight, but looks twenty; he is very fair, with a thin moustache, fine features, a single eyeglass, and the appearance of having been recently taken out of a bandbox.* BENNETT *takes* ARCHIE*'s hand and they go out.*)

BRUCE (*casually*): Hallo, Vincy.

VINCY: Hello, Bruce.

BRUCE: You *will* excuse me, won't you, old boy?

VINCY: Certainly, Bruce. (BRUCE *goes out.*) Edith! (*They embrace.*)

EDITH: Vincy, darling, do sit down. We have good news! Bruce has just told me we're dining Sunday at the Mitchells'.

VINCY: The Mitchells! (*Smiling*) Ah, yes—the Mitchells....

EDITH: How like you, dear Vincy, to know everyone!

VINCY: I've dined there actually. Very amusing people. *Very* amusing.

EDITH: Oh, really? What did they do?

VINCY: Well, the night I was there they played games. And it was all just a *teeny* bit ghastly.

EDITH: Ghastly?

VINCY: Well, the people weren't quite young enough. When they played "Oranges and Lemons and the Bells of St. Clement's," their bones seemed to—well, sort of rattle, if you know what I mean.

EDITH (*laughing*): I think I *do!*

VINCY: Mitchell has such high spirits, you see. He's determined to make everything "go." He insists on plenty of "verve."

EDITH: Verve?

VINCY: They haven't any children, and they make a kind of hobby of entertaining in an unconventional way.

EDITH: It all sounds frightfully amusing. Perhaps *you'll* be asked again next Sunday.

VINCY: I'll call and remind her of me. I daresay she'll ask me.

EDITH: I wonder who'll be there?

VINCY: Anyone might be there. As they say of marriage, it's a lottery.

EDITH: What do you think we'll do?

VINCY: Oh, they might have roulette, or a spiritual *séance*, or a cotillion, or just bridge. You never know. The house is rather like a country house, and they behave accordingly. Even hide-and-seek, I believe, sometimes. And Mitchell adores practical jokes.

EDITH: Well, it *is* rather exciting that we're going to the Mitchells' at last!

VINCY (*archly*): And, my dear Edith, who knows? Perhaps it'll be the turning point of your life!

EDITH (*laughing*): *What* fun—the turning point of my life!... Oh, here's Bruce.

(BRUCE *enters, holding an opera glass.*)

BRUCE: Edith, I don't think much of that opera glass your mother gave you.

EDITH: It's quite the fashion, Bruce. It's jade—the latest thing.

BRUCE: I don't care if it *is* the latest thing. It's no use! Here—try it, Vincy. (*He hands the opera glass to* VINCY, *who tries it.*)

VINCY: Rather quaint and pretty, *I* think. (*He hands the opera glass back to* BRUCE.)

BRUCE: It may be quaint and pretty, and it may be the latest thing. But *I'm* not a slave to fashion. I never was. And I don't see any use whatever in an opera glass that makes everything smaller instead of larger.

EDITH: Bruce, dear—

BRUCE: *I* call it rot. And, Edith, you can tell your mother what I said.

EDITH: Oh, Bruce!

BRUCE: Well, I always say what I think.

EDITH: But, Bruce, dear—you're looking through it the wrong side!

(BRUCE *frowns;* EDITH *and* VINCY *laugh.*)

CURTAIN

Scene Two

Morning. EDITH *is seated at the piano, playing a sentimental tune.*
BRUCE *enters.*

BRUCE: Oh, Edith, dear.

EDITH (*leaving the piano*): Yes, Bruce?

BRUCE: I made a friend last night—a really good friend.

EDITH: *Did* you, dear?

BRUCE: There was one really charming man at the Mitchells',
and he took an immense fancy to me.

EDITH: Oh, really? Who was that?

BRUCE (*mimicking* EDITH): "Oh, really? Who was that?" How
stupid women are in some things! Why, Aylmer Ross, of course.

EDITH (*trying to seem casual*): Aylmer Ross?

BRUCE: Aylmer Ross, the chap who sat next to you at dinner.

EDITH: Oh, yes.

BRUCE: I suppose you didn't appreciate him.

EDITH: Well, actually, Bruce—

BRUCE: *Very* handsome. *Very* clever. An awfully good sort. I
asked him to dine at the club one day—to go on with our conversation.

EDITH: Oh, *did* you?

BRUCE: But it seems he thinks the Carlton's nicer for a talk,
so I'll ask him there instead. *You* can come too, dear. *He* won't
mind.

EDITH: Oh, are we giving a dinner at the Carlton?

BRUCE: Of course we are! Our flat's too small to give a decent
dinner. And Aylmer Ross is one of the nicest chaps I've ever
met.

EDITH: Do you want me to write him, dear?

BRUCE: Uh—no—I've asked him already.

EDITH: Oh, really? Which day?

BRUCE: Well, I suggested next Thursday. But he thought to-night would be better.

EDITH: Tonight!

BRUCE: He's engaged every other night this week.

EDITH: But, Bruce, dear—

BRUCE: Now, Edith, don't go and say you're engaged tonight. If you are, you'll have to chuck it.

EDITH: Oh, no—I'm not engaged.

BRUCE: Tonight, then, it is. At eight o'clock. (*Going*) I say—that Miss Mooney is a very charming person.

EDITH: Miss Mooney?

BRUCE: Myra Mooney—the actress. She took rather a fancy to me, Edith. Uh—you might ask her to dinner too, if you like—to make a fourth.

EDITH: But really, Bruce! Ought we to snatch all the Mitchells' friends the first time?

BRUCE: Why, of course! It's only courteous. One must return hospitality.

EDITH: Shall I telephone her now? It *is* rather short notice, you know.

BRUCE: Oh, Miss Mooney won't care about *that!* To tell the truth, dear, I've asked her already.

EDITH: Already!

BRUCE: So you see, you needn't bother.

(BRUCE *goes out.* EDITH *returns to the piano.* BENNETT *enters.*)

BENNETT (*announcing*): Mr. Aylmer Ross!

(AYLMER ROSS *enters. He is thirty-seven, tall, handsome, gentle-manly.* BENNETT *goes out.* EDITH *rises from the piano and comes forward to greet him.*)

EDITH (*cordially*): Why, Mr. Ross! Good morning! This *is* a surprise! (*She proffers her hand.*)

AYLMER: I hardly know how to apologize, Mrs. Ottley. I oughtn't to have turned up in this cool way. But your husband has kindly asked me to dine with you tonight, and I wasn't sure of the time.

EDITH: The time....

AYLMER: So I thought I'd come and ask.

EDITH: Why, yes!

AYLMER: Of course, if I hadn't been so fortunate as to find you in, I'd have left a note.

EDITH: Oh, I'm glad I'm at home. I felt in the mood to play the piano today. I'm delighted to see you. Won't you sit down? (*They sit down on the sofa.*) It's at eight tonight.... Shall we have coffee?

AYLMER: Oh, no, thanks. I shan't keep you a moment.

EDITH: We had great fun last night, didn't we?

AYLMER: Oh, *I* enjoyed myself immensely—part of the time at least.

EDITH: But after dinner you *were* rather horrid, Mr. Ross. You wouldn't come and talk to me.

AYLMER: I was afraid.

EDITH: Afraid?

AYLMER: Tell me, Mrs. Ottley—do I seem many years older since last night?

EDITH: I don't see any difference. Why?

AYLMER: Because I've lived months—years—since I saw you last.

EDITH: Really?

AYLMER: Time doesn't go by hours, does it?

EDITH: No, I suppose it doesn't.... Aren't the Mitchells dears!

AYLMER: Oh, quite. Do you know them well?

EDITH: Very well indeed. But I've never *seen* them before.

AYLMER: Well—now we've found our way there, we must go and dine with them often, mustn't we, Mrs. Ottley? Can't we go again next week?

EDITH: Very sweet of you to ask us, I'm sure.

AYLMER: Not at all. Very jolly of us to turn up. (*He rises from the sofa and studies some photographs on the table.*) Which is your husband?

EDITH: Over there—opposite—near the end of the table.

AYLMER: Good-looking chap with the light moustache?

EDITH: That's it.

AYLMER (*taking up another photograph*): And this is your boy?

EDITH: Yes, that's Archie. He's six.

AYLMER: I have a boy too. Teddy. Just thirteen.

EDITH: Boys are rather nice things to have about, aren't they?

AYLMER: Tell me about your boy.

EDITH: Oh, I never could talk about Archie!

AYLMER: I'd like to see him…. *May* I see him?

EDITH: Why, yes—of course. But he's out this morning—with his governess.

AYLMER: I saw you speak to Vincy. Dear little fellow, isn't he?

EDITH: Vincy's a great friend of ours.

AYLMER: I'm tremendously devoted to him too. He's what we used to call "an exquisite."

EDITH: Vincy *is* exquisite. He has an exquisite mind.

AYLMER: He seems rather to *look* at life than to *act* in it. He's a brilliant spectator.

EDITH: To Vincy all the world's a stage, and *he's* sitting in the front row of the stalls.

AYLMER: I never could be like that. I want to be onstage in every scene, always performing.

EDITH: Really!

AYLMER: Do you see much of Vincy?

EDITH: Oh, yes. He comes here every day. Or we talk on the telephone.

AYLMER: He asked me last night to go to a tea party at his flat next week. He's asking one or two other "kindred spirits," I think they're called. Including you, of course?

EDITH: I'll certainly go—whether I'm asked or not.

AYLMER (*glancing at the bookshelf*): Tell me, Mrs. Ottley—do you care for books?

EDITH: Oh, yes—rather! I've just been discovering Henry James.

AYLMER: Rather a pompous chap, isn't he?

EDITH: I've just read *The Wings of the Dove* for the first time.

AYLMER: Well, you could do worse than read *The Wings of the Dove* for the first time.

EDITH: I *have* done worse. I've read Rudyard Kipling for the *last* time.

AYLMER: Really? You don't like him?

EDITH: Oh, he's so fearfully familiar with his readers. I feel all the time, somehow, as if he were calling me by my Christian name without an introduction.

AYLMER: Excuse my country manners, Mrs. Ottley, but how nice your husband is! (*He takes up* BRUCE*'s photograph again.*)

EDITH: He liked *you* very much too.

AYLMER: I wonder—does he ever jar on you in any way?

EDITH (*a bit too quickly*): Oh, no. Never. He couldn't. He amuses me.

AYLMER: Oh, does he? If *I* had the opportunity I wonder if *I'd* amuse you.

EDITH: No, I don't think you would.

AYLMER (*laughing*): You mean I'd bore you to death!… Well, I'll see you tonight. At eight.

EDITH: Yes.

AYLMER (*lingering*): What will you wear, Mrs. Ottley?

EDITH: Oh, I thought perhaps my mauve chiffon. (*Smiling*) What do you advise?

AYLMER: Not what you wore last night?

EDITH: Oh, no!

AYLMER: It was very jolly. I liked it. Red, wasn't it?

EDITH (*smiling*): Oh, *no!* It was pink! (*There is an extraordinary pause, during which neither seems able to think of anything to say. There is a curious vibration in the air.* EDITH *glances toward the window.*) Isn't it getting springy! It's one of those warm days that seem to have got mixed up by mistake with winter.

AYLMER (*vaguely*): Yes—very.

(BENNETT *enters.*)

BENNETT (*announcing*): Mr. Vincy!

(VINCY *enters;* BENNETT *goes out.*)

EDITH (*coming forward*): Vincy, darling!

VINCY: Edith.

EDITH: You know Mr. Ross.

VINCY: I do indeed. Hello, Aylmer. (*In mock reproof*) But, Edith, my dear! Really! How *very* soon!

EDITH: Mr. Ross came to know what time we dine. He was just passing.

VINCY (*still jesting*): Oh, yes. He lives in Jermyn Street. I suppose Knightsbridge is on his way home.

AYLMER (*laughing*): After that what can I say? (*Starting to go*) Good-bye, Vincy. Good-bye, Mrs. Ottley.

EDITH (*proffering her hand*): Good-bye, Mr. Ross. You mustn't let Vincy drive you away.

AYLMER (*archly*): Not at all. I see you're occupied. I don't like—to interrupt.

EDITH (*smiling*): Is this a jealous scene, Mr. Ross?

AYLMER (*smiling*): I wonder. And if so, whose…. Well—till eight tonight.

EDITH: Till eight tonight. (*She accompanies* AYLMER *to the door.*) Good-bye!

(AYLMER *goes out. The front door slams and* EDITH *returns.*)

VINCY: My dear Edith, you *did* seem to be getting on *rather* well! (*Archly*) Last night at dinner, I mean.

EDITH: Oh, yes. Aren't the Mitchells amusing!

VINCY: *So* bright. *So* clever. I was sure you'd like them. (*Archly*) And how did you like Aylmer Ross?

EDITH (*trying to seem casual*): Aylmer Ross?

VINCY: Aylmer Ross. He's awfully clever, and awfully nice, and awfully devoted to his boy.

EDITH: Is he really?

VINCY: He married very young, and lost his wife two years after. That was twelve years ago. And he's never looked at another woman since. (*Consolingly*) But he's still quite young, my dear— under forty. And he's sure to fall in love and marry again.

EDITH: Is he really?

VINCY: There's a special fascination about Aylmer. There are so many things he's not.

EDITH: Tell me what he's not.

VINCY: Well, for one thing he's not fatuous.

EDITH: Not fatuous?

VINCY: Though he's so infernally good-looking, he's not a lady-killing sort of person or anything else tedious.

EDITH (*delighted to hear this*): Ah, yes.

VINCY: If he took a fancy to a person—well, it might be rather serious, if you take my meaning.

EDITH: How sweet of him!

VINCY: I suppose he wasn't brilliant today. He was too thrilled.

EDITH: Thrilled?

VINCY: But, Edith, dear—do be just a *teeny* bit careful—because when Aylmer's at all brilliant, he's very much so.

EDITH: What a lot you seem to make of one little visit, Vincy! After all, it was only one.

VINCY: There hasn't been time yet for many more, has there, Edith, dear? He could hardly call twice the same day—on the first day too.

EDITH (*laughing*): Oh, here's Bruce. (BRUCE *enters carrying an enormous basket of flowers.*) Oh, Bruce! How angelic of you!

BRUCE: Don't be in such a hurry, dear. These are not from me. They just arrived at the same time I did. Brought by a commissionaire. There was hardly room for it in the lift.... Hallo, Vincy.

VINCY: Hello, Bruce. *What* a success your charming wife had last night! Everyone was quite wild about her.

BRUCE: Everyone?

VINCY: Quite wild.

EDITH (*reading the card*): It's the minister of that place with a name like Ruritania.

BRUCE: What cheek! What brazen cheek! Upon my word, I've more than half a mind to go and tell him what I think of him—straight from the shoulder. What's the address?

EDITH: Grosvenor Square, I think, dear.

BRUCE: Well, *I* don't care. I'll go straight to the embassy. (*Suddenly*) No, I won't. I'll send them back and write him a line—tell him English women are not in the habit of accepting presents from undesirable aliens.

VINCY: Perhaps he means no harm, Bruce. I daresay it's the custom in that place with the funny name.

BRUCE: Then you don't think I ought to take it up?

EDITH: Not for *me*, certainly. *I* find the basket quite oppressive.

BRUCE: How like you, Edith! I thought you were fond of flowers!

EDITH: So I am, but I like them one at a time.

BRUCE: Some women are *never* satisfied! It's most ungrateful to the poor old man, who meant to be nice and show his respect for English women. I think you ought to write and thank him. And let me see the letter before it goes. (*He goes out.*)

EDITH: Oh, Vincy, darling, do tell me—what will *you* eat tonight?

VINCY: Tonight? Eat? I?

EDITH: Unless you're with other people I can never imagine your sitting down to a proper meal.

VINCY: Oh, I may have a nice apple. Or a nice orange. Or sometimes when I'm alone I just have a nice egg and a glass of water.

EDITH: A nice apple…. A nice orange…. A nice egg.

VINCY: Don't worry about *me*, Edith. *I* get on very well.

EDITH (*laughing*): So I see! Very well indeed! Vincy, my dear, you *must* take better care of yourself. (*Her voice trails off as they go out arm-in-arm.*)

CURTAIN

Scene Three

Afternoon. Edith *is seated at the writing table, pen in hand.* Bennett *enters.*

Bennett: Please, ma'am, would you kindly go into the nursery. Master Archie wants you to hear about the golden—something he's just made up like.

Edith (*rising from the writing table*): Oh, dear! Tell Master Archie I'm coming. (Archie *rushes in.*) Archie, darling!

Archie: Oh, Mother! I *must* tell you about the golden quoribus!

Edith: Why, yes, dear.

Archie (*slowly, in a solemn voice*): The golden quoribus is the most horrible animal, the most awful-*looking* animal, you ever heard of in your life!

Edith: Oh-h-h! How awful! (*Shivering*) The golden quoribus! Let me sit down quietly and hear all about it. (Bennett *goes out.* Edith *sits down and clasps her hands, looking at* Archie *with a terrified expression, which is part of the ritual.*) Much more awful than the gazeka, I suppose?

Archie: Oh, *Mother!* The gazeka's nothing at all! It doesn't count! Besides, it isn't real—it never was real.

Edith: Oh, I *am* sorry! Do go on.

Archie: The golden quoribus is far-ar-r-r-r more frightening even than the jilbery.

Edith: What! Worse than the jilbery!

Archie: And you remember how awful *that* was.

Edith: Oh, good gracious, yes!

Archie: And much larger too.

Edith: How perfectly dreadful! What's it like?

Archie: Well, first of all—it's as long as from here to Brighton.

Edith: Brighton!

ARCHIE: And it's called the golden quoribus because it's bright gold—except the bumps; and the bumps are green.

EDITH: How terrible! And what shape is it?

ARCHIE: All pointed and sharp and three-cornered.

EDITH: Does it breathe fire?

ARCHIE (*staring contemptuously*): Breathe fire! Oh, *Mother!* Do you think it's a silly dragon in a fairy story? How can it breathe fire?

EDITH: Sorry, my dear. Do go on.

ARCHIE: *But*—the peculiar thing is, it lives entirely on muffins and mutton.

EDITH: Muffins and mutton!

ARCHIE: And the *really* frightening part I'm coming to now. (*Becoming emphatic, speaking slowly*) The golden quoribus has more claws than any... other... animal... in the whole... wide... world!

EDITH (*shuddering*): Oh-h-h!

ARCHIE: It has claws coming out if its head.

EDITH: It's head! Good gracious!

ARCHIE: It has claws coming out of its eyes, and claws coming out of its ears, and claws coming out of its mouth!

EDITH: How horrible! How utterly horrible!

(BRUCE *rushes in.*)

BRUCE: Edith, dear.

EDITH: Yes, Bruce?

BRUCE: Aylmer Ross has invited us to dine with him tonight.

EDITH: Aylmer Ross—tonight!

BRUCE: And go on to the theatre afterwards.

EDITH: But, Bruce—

BRUCE: There's no use arguing, Edith. I've already accepted for both of us.

EDITH: But, Bruce—won't your mother be disappointed?

BRUCE: My dear Edith, you can safely leave that to me. Of course she'll be disappointed! But you can go round and see her, and speak nicely and tell her we can't come because we've got another engagement.

EDITH: Am I to tell her it's a subsequent engagement? Otherwise she'll wonder we didn't mention it before.

BRUCE: Don't be in a hurry, dear. Don't rush things. Remember—she *is* my mother.

EDITH: Archie, darling, why don't you go back to Miss Townsend? (*She kisses* ARCHIE.) There—that's a good boy.

(ARCHIE *goes out.*)

BRUCE: Perhaps to *you*, Edith, it may seem old-fashioned. But to *me* there's something very sacred about one's mother.

EDITH: Yes, dear. So don't you think we ought to keep our promise to dine with her? I daresay she's asked one or two people she thinks we might like.

BRUCE: If it comes to that, Aylmer Ross has asked one or two people *he* thinks we might like.

EDITH: But he can't have asked them on purpose, Bruce. We didn't even know him on Sunday.

BRUCE: *How* you argue, Edith! It really seems you're getting absurdly touchy. All those flowers from the embassy must have turned your head. *Why* should he have asked them on purpose? You admit yourself we didn't even know the man last Sunday, and yet you expect— (*He stops, caught in his own tangle.*) Far better, in my opinion—now, don't interrupt me; hear me out—far better, far *kinder,* far more *sensible* for you to sit right down at that little table and take out your stylographic pen and tell my mother I have a bad attack of influenza.

EDITH: Influenza!

BRUCE: One should always be considerate of one's parents. I suppose it's the way I was brought up that makes me feel that way.

EDITH (*sitting down at the writing table*): How bad is your influenza?

BRUCE: Oh, not very bad—because that might really worry her. A slight attack. (*Suddenly*) Stop! Not so very slight. We must let her think it's the ordinary kind, and then she'll think it's catching and she won't come here for a few days, and that will avoid our going into detail.

EDITH: If she thinks it's catching, dear, she'll want Archie and Miss Townsend to go and stay with her in West Kensington.

BRUCE: Right as usual! You're a clever little woman sometimes, Edith. Wait! (*He puts up his hand like a policeman stopping traffic.*) Wait! Leave out the influenza altogether. Just say I've caught a slight chill.

EDITH: But then she'll come over at once, and you'll have to go to bed.

BRUCE: My dear Edith, you're over-anxious. I'll do nothing of the kind. There's no need for me to be laid up for this. It's not serious. (*Beginning to believe in his own illness*) Air! Air! That's what I need! It's the very best thing for a chill. I'll walk down to the club. (*Looking over* EDITH*'s shoulder as she writes*) Ah, that will do very nicely. (*Turning to go*) Good-bye, dear.

EDITH: Good-bye, Bruce.

(BRUCE *goes out.* EDITH *seals her letter, goes to the sofa, takes up a newspaper, and begins to read.* BENNETT *enters.*)

BENNETT (*announcing*): Mr. Aylmer Ross!

(AYLMER *enters;* BENNETT *goes out.*)

EDITH (*putting down her newspaper*): Why, Mr. Ross!

AYLMER: Ah—there you are, Mrs. Ottley—at it again!

EDITH (*laughing*): I know it's very *un*literary of me, but I enjoy newspapers more than anything else in the world.

AYLMER: Tell me exactly—what papers do you read?

EDITH: Four morning papers—never mind their names. Four evening papers. Five Sunday papers.

AYLMER: And how do you find time for all this culture?

EDITH: I read quickly, and what I have to do I do quickly.

AYLMER: Is that why you never seem in a hurry?

EDITH: Well, I do think I've managed to reduce labour-saving to something of a science.

AYLMER: How?

EDITH (*laughing*): By not working, I suppose.

AYLMER (*intensely*): You're wonderful!

EDITH: Do you really think so?

(AYLMER *stands looking out of the window. Suddenly he turns and faces* EDITH.)

AYLMER: It's getting quite decent weather, you know.

EDITH: Yes—quite warm.

AYLMER: I may be going away pretty soon.

EDITH: Going away? But I thought— (*Recovering herself*) It'll be nice weather for you to go away, won't it?

AYLMER: I'll hate it. I'll be miserable.

EDITH: Really!

AYLMER: You're dying to ask me something.

EDITH: Which am I dying to ask you: *where* you're going, or *why* you're going?

AYLMER: I don't know *where* I'm going. But I'll tell you *why*. I'm going because I'm seeing too much of *you*.

EDITH: *Me?*

AYLMER: Seeing you, Mrs. Ottley, is entrancing, but it's also very dangerous.

EDITH: Dangerous?

AYLMER: Well—your company—I'm getting to feel I can't do without it.

EDITH: But why *should* you do without it?

AYLMER: You mean there's no reason why we shouldn't keep on going to plays with Bruce, dining with Bruce, being always with Bruce?

EDITH: But surely you can come and see me now and then?

AYLMER: Oh, that's the worst of all.

EDITH: But why?

AYLMER: I'm not a man who could ever be a "tame cat." And I'm not, I hope, a man who'd dare to spoil—to—

EDITH: Is that why you're going?

AYLMER: You see, Mrs. Ottley, you wouldn't care if you never saw me again.

EDITH: I *would* care! You know, Mr. Ross, we're awfully good friends. I like you immensely.

AYLMER: As much as Vincy?

EDITH: Oh, so differently!

AYLMER: I'm glad of that, at any rate! (*An embarrassed pause.*) So this is really the last time I'm to see you, Mrs. Ottley?

EDITH: But aren't we all dining together tonight—and going to the theatre?

AYLMER: I mean the last time *alone.* Yes, I've got a box for *The Moonshine Girl.* Bruce said you'd come. And Vincy will be there.

EDITH: Oh, that'll be great fun—I love that sort of show.

AYLMER: But tomorrow I'm going away for three months.

EDITH: Three months! A long time.

AYLMER: Will it seem long to you?

EDITH: Why, of course! I'll miss you very much.

AYLMER: Really?

EDITH: We'll *both* miss you very much.

(*They look at each other in silence. There is a strange vibration in the air. Overpowered by sudden impulse,* AYLMER *seizes* EDITH *by the shoulders and kisses her roughly and at random.*)

AYLMER: Edith! I love you, Edith.

EDITH (*resisting*): Oh, Aylmer!

AYLMER: Don't you see, Edith, darling—I can't do without you.

EDITH (*drawing away*): Aylmer, dear—what time do you start tomorrow?

AYLMER: You think I ought to go, then?

EDITH: *You* say so.

AYLMER: But you'd rather I remain here—rather we go on as we are?

EDITH: Yes, Aylmer, I'd rather we go on as we are.

AYLMER: No, Edith—I can't stand it!

EDITH: I should've thought if you liked anyone so *very* much, you'd want to see him all the time, as much as possible—even with other people around.

AYLMER: Edith, dear—you don't know how cruel you are! How do you suppose I feel when I've been out with you—sitting near you, looking at you, delighting in you the whole evening—and then after supper you go away with Bruce?

EDITH (*reproachfully*): Oh, Aylmer!

AYLMER: I must be frank, Edith; we haven't much time.

EDITH: Please, do be frank.

AYLMER: I'd do anything in the world to get you, Edith. I'd do anything in the world to *please* you…. Will you write me?

EDITH: Of course, Aylmer! Of course I'll write you!

AYLMER: And when you write, call me Aylmer. Tell me what you're doing, where you're going, who you're seeing. Tell me about Archie; about your new dresses and hats—any little thing that'll keep us in touch.

EDITH: I shall, Aylmer. I shall. And you must write me too.

AYLMER: Yes—but only officially—only for Bruce…. And listen. Take care of yourself. Do what *you* want sometimes. Don't read too much by electric light and try your eyes. And don't go out in those thin shoes in damp weather. Promise!

EDITH (*smiling*): I promise.

AYLMER: And be a great deal with Archie. I like to think of you with him. And please don't be continually at Vincy's, or at the Mitchells'. I hate for you to be admired!

EDITH: And *I* always thought we'd welcome the "success" of the people we like!

AYLMER: Don't you believe it, Edith! That's all vanity and non-sense. If I can't have you myself, I'd really like you to be shut up. Very happy, very well, with everything in the world you like, but absolutely shut up. And if you did go out, I'd like you to wear a thick veil—and a thick, loose dress.

EDITH (*laughing*): Why, Aylmer—you're quite Oriental!

AYLMER: I'm not a bit Oriental; I'm human. *Human….* Now, is there anything I can do for you while I'm away? Remember—I shan't see you for three months.

EDITH: Don't forget me, Aylmer. I don't want you to forget me. Later on we'll have a real friendship.

AYLMER: *Friendship!* Don't use that word! It's false—it's humbug—for me at any rate. To say I care for you as a *friend* is simply blasphemy! But I'll try. You're an angel—I'll try.

EDITH: And it's horribly inconsistent, and no doubt very wicked of me, but do you know, I'd be rather pained if I heard you'd fallen in love with someone else.

AYLMER: Someone else! Impossible! Never! Never! This is the real thing. There never was anyone like you, Edith, and there never will be. It's *love,* Edith. It's *love.*

EDITH: Dear Aylmer—how sweet!

AYLMER: Let me look at you once more, Edith…. Oh, Edith! (BRUCE *dashes in.*)

BRUCE (*casually*): Oh, hallo, Aylmer.

AYLMER (*recovering himself*): Hello, Bruce.

EDITH: Aylmer's just going.

BRUCE: Going?

AYLMER: Yes, Bruce. I start tomorrow on the Orient Express.

BRUCE: The Orient Express!

EDITH: Doesn't it sound romantic and exciting!

BRUCE (*sighing*): Whether it's romantic and exciting isn't the question, my dear girl. I only wish *we* were going too. But I can't get away from my wretched work to have any fun, like you carefree bachelors.

AYLMER: But I'm *not* a carefree bachelor! My boy is coming to join me for the summer holidays, wherever I am.

BRUCE: Don't you wish we were both going, Edith?

EDITH: Oh, Bruce—surely June's just the nice time to be in London.

AYLMER (*proffering his hand*): Well, good-bye, Bruce. (*He slaps* BRUCE *heartily on the shoulder.*)

BRUCE: Good-bye, old chap.

AYLMER (*proffering his hand*): Good-bye, Edith.

EDITH: Good-bye, Aylmer.

BRUCE (*accompanying* AYLMER *to the door*): We'll see you at half-past seven.

AYLMER: Yes.

EDITH (*calling*): Good-bye!

(AYLMER *goes out. The front door slams, and* BRUCE *returns.*)

BRUCE: It's rather sickening, isn't it—Aylmer's leaving like this. We'll miss him horribly. And then what's the sense, Edith, in a chap leaving London, where he's been all winter, just as it begins to be pleasant?… Yes, Aylmer's a ripping fellow. Do you remember how I pointed him out to you at the Mitchells'? And sometimes when I think how you used to sneer at the Mitchells—oh, you did, you know, before you knew them—and when I remember all the trouble I had to get you to go there, I wonder—I simply wonder! Don't you see—through going there we've made one of the best friends we've ever had?

EDITH: Really, Bruce, you didn't have *any* trouble getting me to go to the Mitchells'. I couldn't go until I was asked. The very first time we were asked, we flew!

BRUCE: Who'll be there tonight, do you know?

EDITH: Only Aylmer and two or three friends and Vincy.

BRUCE: Mind you, I consider *The Moonshine Girl* pure frivolity. But one thing I'll say: a bad show at the Society is better than a good show anywhere else. There's always jolly music, and pretty dresses, and pretty girls. You don't mind my saying so, dear?

EDITH: No, indeed, Bruce. I think so myself.

BRUCE: Of course the first row of the chorus is not what it was when I was a bachelor. Either the girls are not so good-looking, or I don't admire them so much, or they don't admire *me* so much, or—or—something!

EDITH: You're pleased to be facetious.

BRUCE (*putting his arm around* EDITH*'s waist*): My dear girl, you know perfectly well I think there's no one in the world like you. Wherever I go I always say there's no one to touch my wife.

EDITH: Very sweet of you, I'm sure.

BRUCE: But because I think you're pretty, it doesn't follow that

I think everyone else is hideous. I tell you that straight from the shoulder. And I must say this for you, dear—you've never shown any sign of jealousy.

EDITH: Jealousy? I'd show it soon enough if I felt it—if I thought I had any cause!

BRUCE (*laughing*): Oh, don't let's talk nonsense, Edith. Let's go and dress.

(*They go out arm-in-arm.*)

CURTAIN

Act Two

Scene One

Evening. The drawing room is dimly lit. In a moment EDITH *and* BRUCE *enter, still wearing coat, hat, and gloves from the street.* BRUCE *turns on the lights;* EDITH *takes up a letter from the hall table.*

BRUCE: That a letter, Edith?

EDITH: What do you suppose it is, Bruce?

BRUCE: What *could* I suppose it is—a plum pudding?

EDITH: You're very humourous tonight, Bruce.

(BRUCE *removes his hat, slowly draws off one glove, folds it carefully, and puts it down.*)

BRUCE: Letter from a friend?

EDITH (*absently*): What did you say, dear?

BRUCE (*raising his voice*): I said: a letter from a friend?

EDITH: Oh, yes! I heard this time!

BRUCE: Edith, I know of an excellent aurist in Bond Street. I wish you'd go and see him.

EDITH: Bruce, I know of an excellent elocutionist in Oxford Street. I think I'd go and have some lessons if I were you. They teach you to speak clearly—to get your voice over the footlights, as it were.

BRUCE: Edith, are you playing the fool with me?

EDITH (*nodding amiably, in the manner of a person perfectly deaf but pretending to hear*): Yes, dear. Quite right.

BRUCE: What do you mean by "quite right"?

EDITH: Who—me? *I* don't know.

BRUCE (*breezily, in a tone of sudden careless interest*): Who's that letter from, Edith?

EDITH (*in the same tone*): I haven't read it yet, Bruce.

BRUCE: Why don't you read it?

EDITH: Oh, I shall presently.

BRUCE: When?

EDITH: When I've opened it. (BRUCE *draws off his other glove, folds it with the first one, makes them into a ball, and throws it across the room against the window.*) Oh, do you want to have a game? Shall I send for Archie?

BRUCE: Edith, why don't you take off your hat?

EDITH: I can't think. Why don't you take off your coat?

BRUCE: I haven't time. *Show me that letter!*

EDITH: What letter?

BRUCE (*losing his temper*): Don't prevaricate with me, Edith! I can stand anything but prevarication. As if you don't know perfectly well there's only one letter I want to see!

EDITH: Really?

BRUCE: *Who's that letter from?*

EDITH: How should *I* know?

(EDITH *moves toward the door.* BRUCE *goes before and bars the way, standing with his arms outstretched and his back to the door.*)

BRUCE: Edith, I'm pained and surprised at your conduct!

EDITH: Conduct!

BRUCE: Don't echo my words! I'll *not* be echoed, do you hear?… Why don't you wish me to see that letter?

EDITH: Look here, Bruce. I'm thirty-one years old, and I consider you ought to trust me to read my own letters.

BRUCE: Oh, you do, do you? I suppose the next thing you'll wish is to be a suffragette.

EDITH: The question of votes for women hardly enters into our argument here.

BRUCE (*fiercely*): Edith Ottley! *Give me that letter!*

EDITH: Bruce Ottley! Do you think you have the right to speak to me like that?

BRUCE (*pathetically*): Edith, I beg you—I *implore* you: let me see that letter! Hang it all! You know perfectly well, old girl, how fond I am of you. I may worry you a bit sometimes, but you know my heart's all right.

EDITH: Of course, Bruce. I'm not finding fault with you. I only want to read my own letter.

BRUCE: But if you leave this room without showing it to me, then if there's something you don't want me to see, you'll tear it up or chuck it in the fire.

EDITH: It's entirely a matter of principle, dear. We've been married eight years; you leave the housekeeping, Archie's education, and heaps of other things entirely to me; in fact, you lead almost the life of a schoolboy, going to school in the day and amusing yourself in the evening, while everything disagreeable is seen to for you. You won't be bothered even to look at an account.... But I'm not complaining.

BRUCE: Oh, you're not! It sounded a little as if you were.

EDITH: Well, I'm not! I don't *mind* all this responsibility. But I ought at least to be allowed to read my own letters.

BRUCE: Well, darling, you shall—as a rule. I promise you faithfully. Oh, Edith, you're looking awfully pretty tonight; I like that hat. I promise you, dear, I'll *never* ask again—never as long as I live. But I've a fancy to read *that* particular letter. (*Suddenly, fiercely*) What do you suppose is *in* the damned letter? Something you're jolly anxious I shouldn't see!

(EDITH *takes a step forward;* BRUCE *rushes at her and snatches the letter from her hand.*)

EDITH (*indignant*): Bruce!

(BRUCE *tears open the envelope with trembling fingers and reads.*)

BRUCE: "The Lavender Laundry hopes that you will give them a trial, as their terms are extremely moderate—" (*He looks up.*) Oh, Edith!... Edith, dear!... I say, Edith, I *am* sorry. (EDITH *is silent.*) Look here, Edith, I'm just going for a little walk. I'll be back soon.... Don't be angry, Edith. *Please!*

(BRUCE *goes out.* EDITH *removes her coat, hat, and gloves, sits down at the writing table, and begins writing a letter. In a moment* BENNETT *enters.*)

BENNETT (*announcing*): Mr. Vincy!

(VINCY *enters;* BENNETT *goes out.*)

EDITH (*rising from the writing table*): Oh, Vincy, darling!

VINCY: Edith, my dear.

EDITH: You always come just when I need you most!

VINCY: Edith! Has something happened?

EDITH: Last night, Vincy—last night I posted a letter to Miss Townsend.

VINCY: Miss Townsend?

EDITH: Oh, Vincy—it's all too dreadful!

VINCY: Edith, dear, what on earth—?

EDITH: Here is a copy of my letter. Read it for yourself. (*She hands the letter to* VINCY.)

VINCY (*reading*): "Miss Townsend: I've decided Archie's holidays should begin from today." (*He looks up at* EDITH *in consternation.*) "I'm going away with him almost immediately, and I shan't require you any more. Here is a cheque. I shall send your books to your flat in Westbourne Grove." (*He looks up.*) Edith, my dear—?

EDITH: Yesterday afternoon I was walking in Kensington Gardens. I saw, some way off, a girl walking with a man. Her figure was so much like Miss Townsend's I quickened my pace. The two figures turned down a flowery path. I walked on a bit, and I saw it *was* Miss Townsend. She and the man sat down on a bench. He took her hand in his. There was something familiar in his figure, in his clothes. Then I saw his face. It was Bruce!

VINCY: Bruce!

EDITH: Bruce Ottley—seated on a bench in Kensington Gardens holding hands with Archie's governess, Margaret Townsend!

VINCY: My dear Edith—

EDITH: And I had just been thinking what a nice girl she was—what a good friend to me and to Archie!

VINCY: Edith, my dear—*what* a situation!

EDITH: After this, of course, she cannot stay. She has to go. For Archie's sake.

VINCY: My dear Edith, I think you miss Aylmer.

EDITH: Yes, Vincy, I miss Aylmer. He gave a sort of meaning to everything.

VINCY: I had a long letter from Aylmer today.

EDITH: Did you indeed?

VINCY: He seemed *very* unhappy.

EDITH: Bored, is he?

VINCY: Miserable; got the hump; frightfully off colour; wants to come back to London. He misses the Mitchells. (*Archly*) I *suppose* it's the Mitchells.

EDITH (*smiling*): He asked me not to visit you much.

VINCY: Ah—but he wouldn't want you to go *anywhere!* He's not jealous, of course; he's only a little exclusive…. Edith, my dear, I must be going.

EDITH: Oh, Vincy, darling—*must* you go?

VINCY: Just let me know when you need me, and I'll be back.

EDITH: Oh, thank you, my dear! Thank you!

VINCY: Good night, Edith. (*He kisses her on the cheek.*)

EDITH: Good night, Vincy.

(VINCY *goes out.* EDITH *returns to the writing table and continues her letter. In a moment* BRUCE *enters, looking much subdued.*)

BRUCE: Hallo, Edith! (EDITH *is silent; she rises from the writing table.*) How are you, Edith, old girl?

EDITH (*indifferently*): I'm quite well, Bruce.

BRUCE: Edith, I have a sort of idea, you know, that we'll rather miss—uh—Miss Townsend when we go away for the holidays.

EDITH: Bruce—

BRUCE: What do you think of our taking her with us for part of the time?

EDITH (*firmly*): Bruce, we're not taking Miss Townsend with us. She's not coming here any more.

BRUCE: Not coming here any more!

EDITH: Miss Townsend is not coming here any more.

BRUCE: But why? Why? What the devil's wrong?

EDITH: Bruce—

BRUCE: What's the matter with Miss Townsend?

EDITH: Bruce, I prefer not to go into it. And later you'll be glad I didn't. Miss Townsend is not coming here any more. *I'll* look after Archie. It's all settled.

BRUCE: Well, upon my word! (*Eying* EDITH *uneasily*) Have it your own way, of course. But why? Why?

EDITH: Do you really want me to tell you why?

BRUCE: Oh, all right, Edith, dear. After all, you're the child's mother. Have it as you wish.

EDITH: Then we won't discuss it further.

BRUCE: Make whatever arrangements you like. *I* never want to see Miss Townsend again. (EDITH *looks a question.*) And I never shall. (EDITH, *pleased, holds out her hand, which* BRUCE *takes, tears in his eyes.*) Edith, old girl, I think I'll go back to the club.

EDITH: And look here, Bruce—leave it to me to tell Archie.

BRUCE: Whatever you do, Edith, will be— What I mean to say is— Well, good night, Edith. I shan't be long.

(BRUCE *goes out.* EDITH *returns to the writing table and continues her letter. Just as she finishes,* BENNETT *enters.*)

BENNETT (*announcing*): Mr. Aylmer Ross!

(AYLMER *enters;* BENNETT *goes out.*)

AYLMER: Edith, darling!

EDITH (*astonished, overjoyed*): Aylmer! (*She rushes into his arms.*)

AYLMER: It's heavenly being here again.

EDITH: It's heavenly *seeing* you again!

AYLMER: What a time I had away! It got worse and worse.

EDITH: But now you're back.

AYLMER: You're prettier than ever, Edith—prettier and sweeter than ever.

EDITH: But, Aylmer, dear—I've just this moment written you a letter! (*She hands the letter to* AYLMER.)

AYLMER: A letter! (*He opens it eagerly.*)

EDITH: *What* a coincidence!

AYLMER (*reading*): "My dear Aylmer, Darling Vincy was here this evening, and he told me you'd written him saying you weren't so very happy. Oh, Aylmer, why wait till September to come back? Why not come back *now?* I miss you too much. Edith." (*He looks up.*) Where's Bruce?

EDITH: He's gone to the club. He'll be back soon.

AYLMER: Then I won't wait. I'd rather not meet him this evening. When shall I see you again?

EDITH: Oh, I don't know. I can't make plans now.

AYLMER (*with boyish impatience*): Oh, Edith—let me look at you again! (*Intimately*) Do you care for me just a little bit, Edith, darling?

EDITH (*smiling*): You know I do!

AYLMER (*with happy triviality*): Well, what are we going to do about it?

EDITH: Don't talk nonsense, Aylmer. We're just going to see each other now and then.

AYLMER: Well, I'll be satisfied with anything—after what I've suffered not seeing you at all! Let's have a new game. *You'll make* the rules, and *I'll keep* them.

EDITH: Naturally!

AYLMER: How's Archie?

EDITH: Archie's fine. But *I'm* rather bothered.

AYLMER: Bothered?

EDITH: Miss Townsend won't be coming here any more.

AYLMER: Really? I suppose the fool of a girl's engaged or something?

EDITH: She won't be coming here any more.

AYLMER: Will you have to get a new Miss Townsend?

EDITH: I thought of being Archie's governess myself.

AYLMER: But, Edith! That will leave no time for—for—

EDITH: No time for what?

AYLMER: For anything. For *me,* for instance.

EDITH: You just said *I* was to make the rules.

AYLMER: Make them, then. Go on!

EDITH: Well, we'll be intimate friends and meet as often as we can. Once a week you may say you care for me, and I'll say the same. If you find you can't stand it, you'll have to go away again.

AYLMER: I agree to it all—to every word. You'll see if I don't stick to it absolutely.

EDITH: Thank you, dear Aylmer.

AYLMER: Then I mustn't kiss you?

EDITH: No. Never again.

AYLMER: Never again after tonight. (*He takes* EDITH *in his arms and kisses her passionately.*)

EDITH (*sighing*): Now, Aylmer, you must go. I have a lot of worries.

AYLMER (*tenderly*): I never heard you say that before. Can't you give your worries to me?

EDITH: I'll give you nothing more.

AYLMER: Let me demolish them for you.

EDITH: Good-bye, dearest Aylmer. And remember—there are to be no more kisses.

AYLMER (*smiling*): I promise.

(AYLMER *goes out.* EDITH *begins to turn off the lights. In a moment* BRUCE *enters.*)

BRUCE: Hallo, Edith! (*Glancing at* EDITH *cautiously*) I'm just back from the club.

EDITH: So I see.

BRUCE: What have *you* been doing?

EDITH: Aylmer's been here, Bruce.

BRUCE: Aylmer Ross? Didn't know he was back in town.

EDITH: He's only come for a few days.

BRUCE: I'd like to see him. Did he ask after me?

EDITH: Yes.

BRUCE: I suppose you didn't mention—

EDITH: Mention what?

BRUCE: Edith!

EDITH: Yes?

BRUCE (*clearing his throat*): Look here, Edith—I don't mean to blame you in any way for what—uh—arrangements you

make in your own household. But—uh—have you written to
Miss Townsend?

EDITH: Yes. She won't be coming back.

BRUCE: But won't she ask why?

EDITH: I hope not.

BRUCE (*with a tinge of defiance*): Why?

EDITH: Because then I'd have to explain. And I don't like
explaining.

(*There is a pause, during which* BRUCE *takes great interest in his
nails, examining them separately one at a time, then all together, holding
both hands in front of him.*)

BRUCE: Did Archie enjoy his day?

EDITH: Oh, yes.

BRUCE (*suddenly facing* EDITH *with a franker, more manly expression*): Edith, you're a brick. You're too good for me. (EDITH *looks
down and away.*) Look here, is there anything I can do to please
you?

EDITH: Yes, Bruce, there is.

BRUCE: What? I'll do it, whatever it is—on my word of honour.

EDITH: Well, it's a funny thing to ask, but I'd like you to promise
never to see Miss Townsend again. Even by accident. If you meet
her—by accident, I mean—I want you not to see her.

BRUCE: I swear I'll never recognize Miss Townsend even if I
meet her accidentally.

EDITH: I know it's an odd thing to ask. Why should I mind your
seeing Miss Townsend? But I *do* mind, and I'll be grateful.

BRUCE: Then you're not cross, Edith? (EDITH *gives her sweetest
smile.*) Edith! (*With a violent reaction of remorse, and a sort of tenderness, he puts his arm around her; she turns away.*) Don't you forgive
me, Edith?

EDITH: Yes, Bruce, I entirely forgive you. The incident is
closed.

BRUCE: Really forgive me?

EDITH: Absolutely. (*She picks up her coat, hat, and gloves.*) And now—I've had a tiring day and I'm going to bed. (*At the door*) Good night, Bruce.

BRUCE: Good night, Edith.

EDITH: Oh, Bruce—I think there's a letter for you—there on the hall table. It came by the last post.

(EDITH *goes out.* BRUCE *snatches up the letter and tears it open.*)

BRUCE (*reading*): "Dear Mr. Ottley, Of course you know I'm not returning to Archie after the holidays. I'm very unhappy, for I fear I've offended Mrs. Ottley, who's always been very kind to me. May I ask you not to call or write. Mother and I are spending the summer at Bexhill with some friends. Our address will be Sandringham, Seaview Road, Bexhill." (*He looks up.*) Bexhill.... Some boarding house, I suppose. (*He continues reading.*) "I fear I've been rather to blame in seeing you without Mrs. Ottley's knowledge. But you know how one's feelings sometimes lead one to do what one knows one ought not to." (*He looks up.*) What a lot of "one's"! Fine grammar for a governess! (*He continues reading.*) "I'll never forget how happy I was with you and Mrs. Ottley." (*He looks up.*) She's a silly little fool, and I shan't answer. (*He crumples the letter and throws it in the fire.*)

CURTAIN

Scene Two

Morning. EDITH *is seated on the sofa knitting.* ARCHIE *is standing at the window looking out.*

ARCHIE (*turning from the window*): Mother, dear.

EDITH: Yes, Archie?

ARCHIE: Where's Miss Townsend?

EDITH: Miss Townsend's at Bexhill, darling.

ARCHIE: Why is she at Bexhill?

EDITH: I suppose because she likes it.

ARCHIE: Where's Bexhill?

EDITH: In the south of England. East of Brighton.

ARCHIE: Why isn't she Miss Townsend any more?

EDITH: What do you mean, Archie?

ARCHIE: Why isn't she *our* Miss Townsend any more?

EDITH: She's gone away, dear.

ARCHIE: Isn't she coming back?

EDITH: No.

ARCHIE: Is Miss Townsend teaching anyone else?

EDITH: I daresay she is.

ARCHIE: What are their names?

EDITH: How should *I* know, darling?

ARCHIE: Will she teach anyone else called Archie?

EDITH: I suppose it's possible…. Archie, dear—Miss Townsend was very kind to you. But you needn't think about her any more, because you'll be going to school when you come back from the holidays.

ARCHIE (*considering*): Mother, dear—I like you better than Miss Townsend.

EDITH (*laughing*): Very sweet of you, I'm sure!

ARCHIE (*putting his arm around her neck*): You see, you're not a real governess.

EDITH: How do you mean—I'm not a real governess?

ARCHIE: Well, I'm not *obliged* to do what *you* tell me!

EDITH (*laughing*): Oh, *aren't* you!

ARCHIE: Because you're not a real governess, it's more fun for *me*.

(BRUCE *rushes in.*)

BRUCE: Oh, Edith—I've got to go down to Brighton on special business. Right away.

EDITH: Oh, *have* you, Bruce! Brighton!

BRUCE: Look at this wire. (*He reads.*) "Wish to see you at once. If possible come down today. M."

EDITH: Who is "M."?

BRUCE: Mitchell, of course.

EDITH: Mitchell?

BRUCE: Who *should* it be? Mitchell's in Brighton a few days on business.

EDITH: Mitchell….

BRUCE: I may be detained till Tuesday—or even Wednesday.

EDITH: Archie, darling, why don't you go to your room?

ARCHIE: Oh, Mother, *must* I go? Mayn't I stay with you and Father?

EDITH: No, dear—not just now. Run along, and I'll be up soon.

ARCHIE: Yes, Mother. (*He goes out.*)

BRUCE: This is a very nice flat, Edith.

EDITH: What do you mean, Bruce?

BRUCE: I mean it's just the right place for you and Archie. If I were you, I'd stay on here.

EDITH: What do you mean—stay on here? Aren't you coming back?

BRUCE: Me? *What* an idea! Of course I'm coming back! But I've told you—this business of mine—well, it'll take a little time to arrange. Still, I expect to be back on Tuesday…. Or certainly on Wednesday…. Or perhaps sooner.

EDITH: How funny you are, Bruce!

BRUCE: How do you mean—funny? Are you angry with me for

going down to Brighton on special business? Why, here you've got Archie and Vincy and Aylmer and—and my mother. I don't suppose you'll miss me much.

EDITH: Bruce—

BRUCE: You see—uh—this is the sort of business women don't understand.

EDITH: What sort of business?

BRUCE: How do you mean—what sort? It's no particular *sort*. It's just business. (*Suddenly*) Stockbroking—that's what it is! Stockbroking! I want to see a chap who's put me on to a good thing.

EDITH: A good thing....

BRUCE: A *safe* thing. Don't you see? (EDITH *is silent.*) I've explained, haven't I? (EDITH *continues silent.*) Aren't you satisfied?

EDITH: *You* appear to be satisfied, Bruce. But I'm not asking you to give me any details of the business, whatever it may be.... Tell me frankly, Bruce, something I'd like to know.

BRUCE: Are you getting suspicious of me, Edith?

EDITH: Suspicious, Bruce?

BRUCE: That's not like you, Edith. Mind you, it's a great mistake in a woman. Women should always trust. Mistrust sometimes drives a man to—to—

EDITH: To what?

BRUCE: Oh—anyhow it's a great mistake.

EDITH: I only want you to tell me something, Bruce.

BRUCE: Yes?

EDITH: Do you ever see Miss Townsend now?

BRUCE: Never—on my word of honour!

EDITH: And have you never—

BRUCE: Never seen her, never written to her, never communicated with her since she left. Don't know where she is and don't care. *Now* do you believe me?

EDITH: Absolutely. Forgive me for asking.

BRUCE (*going*): I'll write to you, Edith—I'll write to you soon.

EDITH: But, Bruce, dear—you say you'll be back on Tuesday or Wednesday!

BRUCE: Give my love to my mother.

EDITH: Your mother....

BRUCE (*at the door*): I say, Edith—

EDITH: Yes, dear?

BRUCE: Oh—nothing. (*He goes out.*)

CURTAIN

Scene Three

Afternoon. EDITH *is standing at the window, anxious and distraught. A bell rings. She dashes into the hall, where she greets* AYLMER.

EDITH (*offstage*): Aylmer!

AYLMER (*offstage*): Edith, dear.

(*The front door slams, and* EDITH *returns, followed by* AYLMER.)

EDITH (*evidently relieved*): Oh, Aylmer—I *am* glad to see you!

AYLMER: Is Bruce coming back tonight?

EDITH (*laughing ironically*): Bruce? Tonight? From Brighton? Listen to this! (*She takes up a letter.*)

AYLMER: A letter from Bruce?

EDITH: It came this morning. (*Reading*) "Dear Edith, I hope what I'm about to tell you will not worry you too much. Miss Townsend and I are all in all to each other. We've made up our minds to throw in our lot together, and we're starting for Australia today."

AYLMER: Australia!

EDITH (*reading*): "I now ask you, Edith, to give me my freedom as soon as possible. It really is my duty to give my name to Margaret, who is devoted to me heart and soul, and cannot live without me."

AYLMER (*laughing contemptuously*): "Cannot live without me."

EDITH (*reading*): "I shall always have the greatest regard for you, Edith, and wish you well. Believe me, yours affectionately, as always, Bruce." (*She hands the letter to* AYLMER.)

AYLMER (*reading*): "P.S. Vincy will give you all the advice you need." (*He bursts into laughter.*) Good God! This is heavenly! (*He returns the letter to* EDITH.)

EDITH: Heavenly?

AYLMER: Edith, dear—he wants you to set him free!

EDITH: Free?

AYLMER: You'll be free to be my wife!

EDITH: Aylmer, dear—

AYLMER: It's all settled, Edith!

EDITH: You're wrong, Aylmer. I'm not setting him free.

AYLMER: What! Are you mad? Stick to him when he doesn't want you?

EDITH: That remains to be seen. I don't believe everything in that letter. Archie, for instance—

AYLMER: Archie! But he doesn't *want* Archie! He *deserts* Archie!

EDITH: He *is* Archie's father.

AYLMER: If you were married to a criminal who implored you to divorce him, you wouldn't, because he was your son's father?

EDITH: Bruce is not a criminal. He's a fool. He's behaved idiotically, and I can never care for him as I once did. But I mean to give him a chance. I'm not going to jump at his first real folly to get rid of him.

AYLMER: You amaze me, Edith! You're not human! Do you *adore* this man, that you forgive him everything? You don't even seem angry.

EDITH: I *don't* adore him. That's why I'm not angry. I've been terribly hurt. But now I must do what is right.

AYLMER (*shaking his head*): Edith, you don't care for me.

EDITH: Oh, Aylmer—you know I do!

AYLMER: Well, then, it's all right! Fate seems to have arranged this on purpose. You know I'd be good to Archie; I'd do anything on this earth for him. And I'd reconcile Mrs. Ottley to it in ten minutes.

EDITH: I'm not letting Mrs. Ottley know anything about it.

AYLMER: You're not telling her?

EDITH: I'll invent a story to account for his absence. But of course if later—I mean if he persists—

AYLMER: Oh, Edith, don't be a fool! You're throwing away our happiness when you've got it in your hand.

EDITH: Aylmer, dear, there are some things I *can't* do. I can't take advantage of Bruce's folly to smooth the path for myself. What will become of him when they quarrel? He's a good fellow, really. He has no spirit, and not much intellect. But with us to look after him he'll be all right.

AYLMER: *Us!* Edith, I give up understanding you!

EDITH: Let him have his silly voyage…. And I hope *she'll* be seasick!

AYLMER: Then you'll take him back?

EDITH: Yes—officially. He has a right to live in his own house, with his own child.

AYLMER: Edith, you have no pride.

EDITH: Ever since I found out about Miss Townsend, I'm sure I was nice to him, but only like a sister.

AYLMER: Oh, good God! I haven't patience with all this hair-splitting nonsense! Brotherly husbands who leave their wives; sisterly wives who stick to their husbands! (*Suddenly*) Forgive me, Edith. I believe whatever you say is right.

EDITH: You see, it's chiefly on account of the child. If it weren't for Archie, I *would* take advantage of this to be happy with you. At least—no, I'm not sure I would even then. Not if I thought it would ruin Bruce.

AYLMER: And you don't think I'd be good to Archie?

EDITH: Good! You'd be an angel! But I tell you I can't do it.

AYLMER (*in a broken voice*): I won't tease you, Edith. I won't worry you any more. But think what a terrible blow this is to *me*. You show me the chance of heaven, then you voluntarily dash it away. Don't you think you ought to consult someone?

EDITH: I *have* consulted someone. I've consulted *you*.

AYLMER: You take no notice of what I say!

EDITH: As a matter of fact, I've made my own decision. And I've written my letter. (*She takes the letter from the writing table.*)

AYLMER: I suppose you won't let me read it?

EDITH: No, Aylmer—you *shall* read it. You *shall* read it because I trust you—I really trust you. (*She hands the letter to* AYLMER.)

AYLMER (*reading*): "Dear Bruce, I'm not going to reproach

you, and I'm not going to make any appeal to your feelings; for if you don't sense the claims of others on you, my words will make no difference.

"I propose to do nothing at all for three months. If in three months you write to me still desiring to be free, I'll think of it, though I'm not sure I'll do it even then. But in case you change your mind I propose to tell nobody, not even your mother. By the time you get this letter, it will be six weeks since yours to me. Perhaps by then you'll be glad to hear I've told your mother merely that you've been ordered away for a change; and I'll say the same to anyone else who inquires for you.

"I'll regard it all as an unfortunate aberration. And if you regret it, and change your mind, you'll be free at any time to come back, and nothing will ever be said. Should it become a question of money, as so many things do, I'll help you. If you really find happiness in the way you expect, we can arrange it. You see, I've thought of everything in one day. Edith Ottley."

(AYLMER *returns the letter to* EDITH.)

EDITH: And now—let's be happy for the rest of the summer.

AYLMER: Edith Ottley—you're incredible! You're absolutely priceless!… I'll help you, Edith, dear. I'll do whatever you wish. I see there's still hope.

EDITH: Hope?

(BENNETT *enters.*)

BENNETT (*announcing*): Mr. Vincy!

(VINCY *enters;* BENNETT *goes out.*)

EDITH (*coming forward*): Vincy, darling!

VINCY: Edith!

AYLMER: Vincy, old boy!

VINCY: Aylmer…. You know, Edith, I've been wondering—whatever happened to Miss Townsend?

EDITH: I hear Miss Townsend's run away with a married man.

VINCY: Never, Edith! Who would've thought it! It's too good to be true!

EDITH: Don't say that, Vincy.

VINCY: But how did you hear it?

EDITH: I heard it on good authority. I *know* it's true.

VINCY: And who's the poor dear man?

EDITH: Bruce was always inclined to be romantic, you know.

VINCY: Oh, give over!

EDITH: I didn't want anyone to know. I'm so afraid of making Mrs. Ottley unhappy.

VINCY: But you're not serious, Edith!

EDITH: I suppose I'd better show you his letter, Vincy. He tells me to ask your advice. (*She hands the letter to* VINCY, *who goes to the window and stands reading it to himself.*)

AYLMER: Well, Edith, I'll be off. Good-bye, Vincy.

VINCY: Good-bye, Aylmer.

AYLMER: Good-bye, Edith, dear. May I see you tomorrow?

EDITH: Come for tea. Four o'clock?

AYLMER: Four o'clock.

EDITH: Good-bye, Aylmer.

(AYLMER *goes out.* VINCY *returns the letter to* EDITH.)

VINCY: Well, I'm gormed! Simply gormed! That's really the only possible word—*gormed!*

EDITH: It's strange, Vincy, but I'm not a bit jealous. I still have a sort of pity for Bruce—almost like a mother. So I'm giving him a chance.

VINCY: But what about Aylmer?

EDITH: Aylmer?

VINCY: Really, Edith, I think Aylmer ought to go away.

EDITH: Go away?

VINCY: It's a mistake to let him stay here and suffer.

EDITH: Dear Vincy, I don't agree. If I were taking Bruce at his word, it would be different, of course.

VINCY: It does seem a pity not to. Everything would then be all nicely settled—just like the fourth act of a play.

EDITH: How can life be like a play?

VINCY: Edith, do you think if Bruce knew how much you like Aylmer he'd have written that letter?

EDITH: No. And I don't believe he'd ever have gone away.

VINCY: Still, I think you ought to send Aylmer away now.

EDITH: My dear Vincy, nothing could be more intensely correct. Why shouldn't I have the pleasure of seeing Aylmer when Bruce is having a heavenly time on board ship?

VINCY (*gently*): Edith, dear—are you unhappy?

EDITH: No, Vincy, I'm not a bit unhappy—now. Once I've taken a line—no matter what it is—I can be happy again.

VINCY: You can adjust yourself to your good fortune.

EDITH: Now that I'm over the shock and pain of Bruce's letter, I'm happier than ever before.

VINCY (*laughing*): You know, Edith—Bruce must be an even bigger bore than I thought!

EDITH: Well, I know I've done the right thing.

VINCY: Yes, my dear, you've done the right thing. And you've done the *wise* thing. (*His voice trails off as they go out together.*)

CURTAIN

Scene Four

Early evening. EDITH *and* AYLMER *are seated on the sofa having tea.*

AYLMER: Edith, darling.

EDITH: Yes, Aylmer?

AYLMER: You've had another letter from Bruce.

EDITH: Yes, Aylmer, I've had another letter from Bruce.

AYLMER: Go on, dear—don't keep me in suspense!

EDITH: Well, they've quarrelled.

AYLMER: Quarrelled!

EDITH: They quarrelled so frightfully on board ship that a young man interfered. As soon as they arrived in port she and the young man were married.

AYLMER: Married!

EDITH: A commercial traveller. Only twenty-five. It seems he pitied her so much he proposed to her on board.

AYLMER: And Bruce?

EDITH: Bruce is relieved I've not told anyone. Now Archie will never know. But I've told Mrs. Ottley everything. I thought I'd better, now it's over. She won't ask questions.

AYLMER: But *is* it over?

EDITH: Bruce got home last night.

AYLMER: My God! He's already back!

EDITH: Yes, Aylmer, he's already back.

AYLMER (*bitterly*): That's right, Edith! Forgive him again! *And* again! *And* again! Would you have done that for *me*?

EDITH: Oh, no, Aylmer—never! If you'd been unfaithful, I'd never have forgiven you.

AYLMER: But why?

EDITH: Because I care for you too much. If you had been in

Bruce's position I'd never have seen you again. With him it's different. I feel no jealousy; I feel no passion. I can judge calmly.

AYLMER (*bitterly*): All right! All right! Judge calmly! Do the right thing! *You* know best! I understand now. I see clearly at last. You've had the opportunity and you wouldn't take it. You don't care for me. I'm going. (*He goes to the door.*)

EDITH: Oh, come back, Aylmer! Don't go like that! You *know* I care for you! But what could I do? I couldn't make my happiness out of someone else's misery.

AYLMER: And you think he'll alter now—be grateful and devoted?

EDITH (*shaking her head*): Do people alter?

AYLMER: Oh, Edith, *I* could make you happy! How could you torture me like this?

EDITH: I don't mean to torture you. We enjoy being together.

AYLMER: But that only makes it harder.

EDITH: It would be such a risk!

AYLMER: But is anything worth having if you're not ready to risk everything to get it?

EDITH: I *would* risk everything—for myself. But not for others. But please, Aylmer—if you feel you must go away, let it be only for a little while.

AYLMER: A *little* while! I hope I never see you again! Do you think I could ever be a "tame cat"? You forget I'm a man! (EDITH *bursts into tears.*) You've been cruel to me, Edith—and you're too good for *him. I've* been the victim, that's all.

EDITH: But won't you be friends?

AYLMER: No. I won't and I can't…. If you'll change your mind, we can still be happy. Give him up, Edith! *Give him up!*

EDITH: Aylmer, darling, I can't! I simply can't!

AYLMER: Then—this is good-bye.

EDITH: Oh, Aylmer—no! (AYLMER *seizes her by the shoulders and kisses her passionately. Then he goes out.* EDITH, *dazed and distraught, falls on the sofa and sobs convulsively.*) No!… No!… Oh, Aylmer!… No!

(Bruce *rushes in.*)

Bruce: Edith, dear!

Edith (*trying to collect herself*): Yes, Bruce?

Bruce: Edith— (*Seeing* Edith's *distraught state*) Oh, Edith—is everything all right?

Edith (*sighing*): Yes, Bruce—everything is all right.

Bruce: Oh, splendid! Now, Edith—

Edith: Aylmer Ross was here. He's leaving London again—this time, he says, for good.

Bruce: For good! Fancy that!… Edith, dear.

Edith: Yes, Bruce?

Bruce: What are you wearing tonight?

Edith: Tonight? Oh—anything.

Bruce: Don't say *anything*, Edith. I don't want you to wear *anything*. I'm anxious you should look your best—especially as we haven't been to the Mitchells' for so long.

Edith: Very well, Bruce.

Bruce (*admiring himself in the glass*): I see *I'm* a bit sunburnt. But it doesn't suit me badly, does it?

Edith: Not at all, Bruce.

Bruce: Edith, dear—we'll be late!

Edith: We shan't be late, Bruce. We're invited for eight o'clock, and eight o'clock I suppose means—well, eight o'clock. Sure you've got the time right?

Bruce: *Really*, Edith! My memory is perfect! I never make a mistake. Haven't you noticed?

Edith: Yes, Bruce—I think I have.

Bruce: Now, Edith, dear—you must be perfectly at ease to-night—absolutely natural.

Edith: Yes, Bruce.

Bruce: And it doesn't matter a bit what you wear, as long as you put on your best dress.

Edith: Yes, Bruce.

Bruce: And anyhow, Mrs. Mitchell isn't the sort of person

who'd think any less of a pretty woman for being dowdy and out of fashion.

EDITH: Yes, Bruce.

BRUCE: Edith, dear.

EDITH: Yes, Bruce?

BRUCE: If I've spoken of it once, I've spoken of it forty times! That inkstand is too full!

EDITH: I'll see to it, Bruce.

BRUCE: Don't let me have to speak of it again, Edith.

EDITH: Of course, Bruce.

BRUCE: I wonder who'll be at the Mitchells' tonight?

EDITH: Oh, I suppose there'll be that new person—the woman with the foghorn voice. And of course the usual people: Mr. Cricker, Miss Mooney—

BRUCE: Miss Mooney! I hope not! I can't stand that woman!… And— Edith!

EDITH: Yes, Bruce?

BRUCE: I don't want to interfere between mother and son—I know you're perfectly capable of bringing up the boy. But lately Archie's got a way of answering back that I don't like at all. Speak to him about it, won't you, Edith?

EDITH: Oh, yes, dear—of course I will.

BRUCE: I know it isn't for *me* to interfere. I've always made a point of letting you do exactly as you like with the boy. But I'm beginning to think Archie ought to have another governess—

EDITH: Oh, he's only six, Bruce—still quite a baby. I daresay I can manage him for the present. Leave it to me.

BRUCE: Oh, Edith, London in the summer will be *such* a bore without Aylmer Ross! *So* dull! This sudden mania on Aylmer's part for long journeys is most annoying. Why do you think he's gone away?

EDITH: I haven't the slightest idea, Bruce.

BRUCE: Do you know, Edith, it's occurred to me that if—well, if things had turned out differently, and you had done as I *asked* you—

EDITH: Yes, Bruce?

BRUCE: I have a sort of idea Aylmer might—well, might have proposed to *you!*

EDITH: *What* an extraordinary idea!

BRUCE: But he never showed any sign, I suppose, of—well, of being more interested in you than he ought to have been?

EDITH: Good heavens, no!

BRUCE: Of course you're not his style. But you liked him very much, didn't you, Edith?

EDITH: I like him very much now.

BRUCE: But I doubt if you ever quite appreciated him. Aylmer is more a man's man. *I* miss him, of course; he's a very great friend of mine. And he never in the least seemed to—?

EDITH: Seemed to what?

BRUCE: It would've been a very unfair advantage to take of my absence if he had.

EDITH: Oh!

BRUCE: But he was incapable of it, of course.

EDITH: Of course.

BRUCE: He never showed any special interest, then, beyond—?

EDITH: Never.

BRUCE: I was right, I suppose. As usual. You never appreciated him, Edith. But then he's not the sort of man a woman *would* appreciate. Do you know, Edith—somehow I felt all along Aylmer wouldn't stay. Isn't it odd! I often think I'm a pessimist. I suppose I'm really a fatalist. Sometimes I hardly know *what* I am.

EDITH (*at the door*): *I* could tell you what you are, Bruce. But I won't. (*She goes out, leaving* BRUCE *staring in bewilderment.*)

CURTAIN

Love at Second Sight

Love at Second Sight, a comedy in two acts, is drawn from the novel *Love at Second Sight,* by Ada Leverson, first published in London in 1916.

CHARACTERS

EDITH OTTLEY

ARCHIE OTTLEY

BRUCE OTTLEY

BENNETT

MADAME FRABELLE

SIR TITO LANDI

AYLMER ROSS

SCENES

Time: 1916

Place: London

The scene is set in the drawing room of the
Ottley house in Cadogan Place

ACT ONE

Scene 1	Afternoon
Scene 2	Morning
Scene 3	Afternoon

ACT TWO

Scene 1	Morning
Scene 2	Afternoon
Scene 3	Afternoon
Scene 4	Morning

Act One

Scene One

The drawing room of the Ottley house in Cadogan Place, London. Afternoon. It is a comfortable, pleasant, informal room agreeably furnished. A fire is burning on the hearth.

At rise EDITH OTTLEY, *aged thirty-five, intelligent, charming, and very pretty, is seated on the sofa knitting. In a moment she hears offstage an appalling crash, followed by piercing shrieks, a loud, unequal quarrel on a staircase, and the bang of a door.*

EDITH (*calling*): Archie! Archie! What's that noise? Archie! Come here at once! (ARCHIE OTTLEY, *a nice-looking boy aged ten, walks calmly into the room.*) Archie Ottley! What was that noise?

ARCHIE: It wasn't *me* that made the noise. It was Madame Frabelle.

EDITH: Madame Frabelle!

ARCHIE: It wasn't *my* fault. It was *her* fault.

EDITH: Now, Archie—

ARCHIE: Madame Frabelle said *she'd* teach me to take away her mandolin and use it for a cricket bat. She needn't teach me; I already know.

EDITH: Now, Archie—you've no right to go into Madame Frabelle's room when she isn't there.

ARCHIE: How can I go in when she *is* there?

EDITH: You oughtn't to go into Madame Frabelle's room without her permission.

ARCHIE: It isn't *her* room; it's *your* room. At least, it's the spare room.

EDITH: Have you done any harm to the mandolin?

ARCHIE (*hesitating*): Uh—no. No harm.

EDITH: Well, Archie, what have you done?

ARCHIE: I can mend it.

EDITH: Madame Frabelle has been very kind to you, Archie. I'm sorry you're not behaving nicely to a guest in your mother's house. It isn't the act of a gentleman.... Now, go and say you're sorry.

ARCHIE: Will it be the act of a gentleman to say I'm sorry? It'll be the act of a story-teller, you know.

EDITH: What! Aren't you sorry you bothered Madame Frabelle?

ARCHIE: I'm sorry she found out.

EDITH: These perpetual scenes between my son and my guest are most painful to me.

ARCHIE: Well, she needn't have quarrelled.

EDITH: But isn't she very kind to you?

ARCHIE: Oh, she isn't bad sometimes. I like it when she tells me lies—I mean stories—about her husband.... Is she a homeless refugee?

EDITH: Not exactly, my dear. She's a widow, and she's staying with us, and we must be nice to her.

ARCHIE: But, Mother—

EDITH: I think I'd better go up and see her.

ARCHIE: Oh, Mother—I shouldn't if I were you!

EDITH: Now, go and do something useful, Archie.

ARCHIE: But, Mother—it's almost the end of my holidays!

EDITH: That's no reason why you should spend your time smashing the musical instruments of guests in your mother's house.

ARCHIE: But, Mother—Madame Frabelle isn't *poor*. She gave me sixpence the other day for not being frightened of a cow.

EDITH: That only proves she's kind. And I didn't say she's poor. That's not the point. We must be nice to anyone staying with us.

ARCHIE: I say, Mother, are all foreigners bad-tempered?

EDITH: Madame Frabelle is not a foreigner.

ARCHIE: But her husband was. He used to get into frightful rages. Do you suppose she talked English to him?

EDITH: That's quite enough, Archie. Now, go and find something to do.

ARCHIE (*at the door*): Mother!

EDITH: Yes, darling?

ARCHIE: Does Father like Madame Frabelle?

EDITH: Why, yes, dear—of course he does.

ARCHIE: *How* funny! Well, I'll say I'm sorry—when I see her again.

(BRUCE OTTLEY, *aged thirty-seven, tall, good-looking, and well built, enters.*)

EDITH: Oh, hello, Bruce, dear.

BRUCE: Hallo, Edith. Hallo, Archie.

ARCHIE: Hello, Father.

EDITH: Now, run along, Archie, darling. It's time for your tea. (*She kisses* ARCHIE.) And I must speak with Father. (ARCHIE *goes out.*) Well, Bruce—about that delicate matter you wished to talk over with me.

BRUCE: Edith, dear—before we get into that, you could do me a really great service by helping me find a certain book.

EDITH: Why, of course, Bruce—with pleasure. What is the book?

BRUCE: *What is the book!* My dear Edith, don't you see I shouldn't have come to you if I knew what the book was.

EDITH: I beg your pardon, Bruce. But if you can't give me the name of the book I scarcely see how I can find it.

BRUCE: And if I knew its name I shouldn't want your assistance!

EDITH (*going to the bookcase*): Can't you give me some idea of what it's like?

BRUCE: Certainly I can. I've seen it a hundred times in this very room.

EDITH: Is it a novel?

BRUCE: No.

EDITH: Is it blue?

BRUCE: No.

EDITH: Does it belong to the library?

BRUCE: No.

EDITH: Is it French?

BRUCE: No.

EDITH: Is it suitable for children?

BRUCE: Suitable for children! Do you think I'd take all this trouble to come and ask your assistance looking for a book that's suitable for children?

EDITH: But, Bruce, if you ask my assistance without giving me the slightest idea of what book it is, how can I possibly help?

BRUCE: Quite so, Edith. Quite so. Never mind. Don't trouble. If I say it's a pity there isn't more order in this house you won't regard it, I hope, as a reproach in any way. If there were a place for everything, and everything were in its place— But never mind, dear. I don't blame *you*. Not in the least. Still, when Archie grows up I'll be sorry if—

EDITH: Oh, Bruce, it's nothing to do with order! It's a question of your memory. You don't remember the name of the book.

(*At this moment* BRUCE *decides it is time to find the book; he suddenly springs at the writing table and seizes a volume triumphantly.*)

BRUCE: There it is! There it is! Staring at you the whole time! Oh, Edith! Edith! How like a woman! And the very book a few inches from your hand! I hope, dear, in future you'll be more careful.

EDITH (*examining the book*): Need I point out, Bruce, that your book *is* a novel? And it's blue, and it belongs to the library, and it's French, and it's still suitable for children.

BRUCE (*laughing nervously*): Well, well. Here it is! Well, well.... And now for the point I was about to make.

EDITH: Shall we have tea, dear?

BRUCE: Oh, surely not. It's only just four. I don't think it's good for the servants to have tea half an hour earlier than usual. Besides—as a matter of fact, I've already had tea at the club.

EDITH (*ringing the bell*): And now for the point—

BRUCE: I'll tell you, Edith, after Bennett has gone.

EDITH: Oh, can't you tell me *now*?

BRUCE: Before I say any more—where is Madame Frabelle?

EDITH: Madame Frabelle's in her room. She stays there a good deal, you know.

BRUCE (*admiring himself in the glass*): What does she do there?

EDITH: She says she goes there to read. She thinks it bores people to see a visitor sitting about the house with a book.

BRUCE: She can't be reading all those hours, surely? (*He sits down, satisfied with his appearance.*)

EDITH: I used to think she was probably lying on the sofa with cold cream on her face. Once I went in and found her doing Swedish exercises.

BRUCE: Good heavens! Do you mean to say she's learning Swedish on top of all those other languages she knows?

EDITH: No, no, Bruce. I mean *physical* exercises. (BENNETT *enters carrying the tea tray and places it before* EDITH.) Thank you, Bennett. (BENNETT *goes out.*) But go on, Bruce. I'm getting impatient!

BRUCE: I never dreamt, Edith—

EDITH: Oh, Bruce—are you going to tell me everything you never dreamt? We'll take weeks getting to the point!

BRUCE: Then I'll get to the point at once. I think we ought to give a dinner for Madame Frabelle.

EDITH (*relieved*): Oh, is *that* all? Of course! I've been wondering why you didn't wish to do it long before now.

BRUCE: I'll tell you why. Thinking Madame Frabelle was a friend of Lady Conroy, it stood to reason she already knew everyone in London—that is, everyone *worth* knowing. But I found out, only last night—what do you think?

EDITH: I *can't* think!

BRUCE: Why, she isn't an intimate friend of Lady Conroy at all! She only made her acquaintance two days before she came to London!

EDITH (*laughing*): Then why on earth did Lady Conroy send her to us with a letter of introduction?

BRUCE: Because she likes us. And she never said she'd known her all her life. We jumped to that conclusion.

EDITH: And how did you find out?

BRUCE: Yesterday evening, when you went up to Archie and left me alone with Madame Frabelle, she told me herself. She's always like that, you know—so frank and open.

EDITH: I hope you didn't let her think—

BRUCE: Edith! As if I *would*!... Well, that being so, I want to ask some people to meet her.

EDITH: She seems very happy with us alone, doesn't she?

BRUCE: But I don't want her to think we don't know anyone. And it seems a bit selfish too—keeping her all to ourselves.

EDITH: And who do you want her to meet?

BRUCE: I want her to meet the Mitchells. It's only a chance, of course, she hasn't met them here already. And I've told Mitchell at the Foreign Office a good deal about her.

EDITH: And then the Mitchells will ask her to their house, of course.

BRUCE: Well, it's a very pleasant house, you know. And she likes celebrities and clever people and that sort of thing.

EDITH: Mrs. Mitchell will count *her* as one, no doubt.

BRUCE: I daresay. But so she is.

EDITH: I know she is—in a way. But, Bruce, don't you wonder why she stays here so long? I mean—there's no question of its being for—well, for reasons of *convenience*. She has a far larger income for herself than we have altogether.

BRUCE: How do you know?

EDITH: She showed me her bankbook one day.

BRUCE: Why did she do that?

EDITH: Perhaps she wanted me to know how she's placed. She's really quite generous—even extravagant, I should say.

BRUCE: Quite so. Still, it's comfortable here, and saves her trouble. And she likes us.

EDITH: I think she does.

BRUCE: Well, *I* don't mind her being here. It's a nice change.

EDITH: But it does seem odd she hasn't said a word about going.

BRUCE: Well, about the dinner. Let it be a small, intimate dinner. She likes a chance to talk.

EDITH: She does indeed. All right, Bruce, you can leave it to me. We'll have eight people, shall we?

BRUCE: And she must sit next to me—on my left. And *not* lilies of the valley—she doesn't like the scent.

EDITH: But, Bruce, dear—what was that delicate matter you wished to talk over with me?

BRUCE: Ah, I was just coming to that.... Hush!

(*Suddenly* MADAME FRABELLE *enters, dressed in a violet tea gown. She is a handsome, statuesque woman aged fifty—graceful, dignified, charming, with extraordinary personal magnetism. She speaks English without a trace of continental accent.*)

EDITH: Ah, Eglantine, my dear!

MADAME FRABELLE (*all smiles*): Edith, darling! *And* Mr. Ottley!

BRUCE (*all punctilio*): Good afternoon, Madame Frabelle!

MADAME FRABELLE: *How* lovely!

EDITH (*holding out a cup*): Tea?

MADAME FRABELLE: Oh, yes, indeed, my dear! I'm always ready for tea. Everything else I can do without. But a cup of tea in the afternoon is an absolute *necessity*. (*She sits down.*) And you have such delightful tea, my dear! (BRUCE *hands her a cup of tea.*) Oh, thank you, Mr. Ottley! It's nice to see you back from the office so early.

BRUCE: Wouldn't you like a slice of lemon?

MADAME FRABELLE: Oh, no, Mr. Ottley! Cream and sugar for *me*, please.

(BRUCE *brings* MADAME FRABELLE *cream and sugar.*)

EDITH: My dear Eglantine—I'm afraid Archie's been bothering you today.

BRUCE (*horrified*): What—Archie!

MADAME FRABELLE: Oh, no, no, no! Not the least in the world, Mr. Ottley! No, no. Archie's a most delightful boy. We were only having a little fun together—about my mandolin.

EDITH: But those sounds I heard on the stairs?

MADAME FRABELLE: Oh, I'm afraid I *did* get just a wee bit cross—a thing I very seldom do. But we've quite made it up now…. Oh—and by the way, I do want to speak to you both rather seriously about your boy.

BRUCE: About our boy?

MADAME FRABELLE: About your boy. Do you know, Mr. Ottley, I have a very curious gift. I can always see in children what they'll make a success of in life. Without boasting, I must say I'm an extraordinary judge of character.

BRUCE: Jolly good!

MADAME FRABELLE: Oh, I've always been like that.

EDITH: Have you indeed?

MADAME FRABELLE: *I'll* tell you what you must make of your boy.

EDITH: Please *do!*

MADAME FRABELLE (*as if announcing a great discovery*): Your boy is a born musician!

EDITH (*incredulous*): A born musician!

MADAME FRABELLE: That boy's a born composer! He has a profound gift for music. Look at his broad forehead! And those grey eyes, so wide apart! Why go against nature? The boy's a genius!

EDITH: But—Archie hasn't the slightest ear for music!

BRUCE: He dislikes music intensely—he simply loathes it!

EDITH: He cried so much over his piano lessons we had to give them up. It used to make him quite ill—and his music mistress too. I remember she left the last time in hysterics.

BRUCE: Yes, by Jove! Pretty girl she was.

EDITH: Oh, no, dear—you're thinking of the other one—the girl who tried to teach him the violin.

MADAME FRABELLE: Nothing on earth to do with it, my dear! The boy's a born composer!

BRUCE: Really! Funny he hates it so. Still, I have no doubt—

MADAME FRABELLE: Believe me, you can't go by his not liking his lessons. The young Mozart—

EDITH: Mozart! I thought Mozart played the piano when he was only three.

MADAME FRABELLE: Handel, I mean. Or was it Meyerbeer? At any rate, you'll see I'm right.

EDITH: You really think we ought to force Archie against his will to study music, with the idea of his being a composer when he grows up, even though he detests it?

MADAME FRABELLE: Even though he detests it!

BRUCE: But, Madame Frabelle—

MADAME FRABELLE: Won't you feel proud, Mr. Ottley, when you see your son conducting his own opera—to the applause of thousands!

BRUCE: Well, I must say—

MADAME FRABELLE: Won't it be something, Edith, to be the mother of the greatest composer of the twentieth century!

EDITH: Well, it *would* be rather fun.

MADAME FRABELLE: We shan't be hearing quite so much about Strauss and Debussy and Elgar and all *those* people once Archie Ottley grows up!

BRUCE: I don't hear much about them now.

EDITH: Well, my dear, how *should* you—at the Foreign Office?

BRUCE: Perhaps he'll turn out to be another Victor Herbert!

MADAME FRABELLE (*shaking her head gravely*): Oh, *dear,* no! It'll be music of the very highest class—the top of the tree—the real thing!

BRUCE: Edith, dear, Madame Frabelle may be right!

MADAME FRABELLE: *May* be right! I *know* I'm right! No question about it!

EDITH: Well, what do you think we ought to do about it? Archie goes to a school now where there's no music at all.

MADAME FRABELLE: So much the better! The sort of music he'd get at school would be no use whatever.

EDITH: So I should think.

MADAME FRABELLE: Leave it, say, for the moment, and when he comes back for the next holidays put him under a good teacher—a really great man. And you'll see!

BRUCE: Funny, though, isn't it—his not knowing one tune from another when he's a born musician.

(BRUCE *goes out, shaking his head.* MADAME FRABELLE *draws her chair nearer* EDITH.)

MADAME FRABELLE: Edith, my dear, I'm longing to tell you something. You've been very kind to me, and I look upon you as a real friend.

EDITH: That's very sweet of you, my dear.

MADAME FRABELLE: Speaking frankly, Edith, I *see* something. I see something very serious.

EDITH: Indeed?

MADAME FRABELLE: Edith, my dear, you're not *quite* happy.

EDITH (*smiling*): Not happy?

MADAME FRABELLE: Not *quite* happy. You have a trouble, and I'd give *anything* to take it away! (*She presses* EDITH*'s hand in sympathy, then looks away.*)

EDITH (*amused*): What do you think I'm unhappy about?

MADAME FRABELLE: My dear Edith, you're beginning to feel the dawn of love.

EDITH: The dawn of *love!*

MADAME FRABELLE: For someone very close.

EDITH: Indeed!

MADAME FRABELLE: *And,* my dear—you're struggling very hard against it.

EDITH: May I ask—who this "someone" is?

MADAME FRABELLE: I haven't met him yet. But isn't there a

name I hear quite often? Something tells me it's— Yes! I'll know as soon as I see him.

EDITH: Are you referring to—?

MADAME FRABELLE: Yes—to Mr. Mitchell!

EDITH (*still amused*): Mr. Mitchell!

MADAME FRABELLE: My dear Edith, you can't hide it from *me!*

EDITH: But, Eglantine—

MADAME FRABELLE (*shaking her head*): Alas, alas, it's always the husband's great friend! Oh, my dear—I've seen so much! *So much!...* Now, *I'm* going to help you. I'm determined to leave you two charming people without a cloud when I go.

EDITH: You're not thinking of *going!*

MADAME FRABELLE: Not yet, my dear. Not yet. I've many, many friends in London, and many, many friends in the country. But I haven't looked them up; I've been too happy *here*. And I'm so interested in *you!*

EDITH: That's very sweet of you, my dear.

MADAME FRABELLE: And another thing, Edith—may I say? —for I feel I've known you for years. You *think* your husband doesn't know. But you're wrong!

EDITH: Am I really!

MADAME FRABELLE: Last night a certain look when he spoke of the Mitchells showed me Bruce is terribly jealous.

EDITH: Jealous!

MADAME FRABELLE: He doesn't show it yet, but he is.

EDITH: But—*Mrs.* Mitchell. She's one of our best friends—a dear thing.... We're lunching there, you know, on Tuesday.

MADAME FRABELLE: I'm delighted to hear it. I'll understand everything then. But even without seeing them I know all about it. Isn't it odd!

EDITH: Isn't it!

MADAME FRABELLE: I think I have a touch of second sight.

EDITH: But, Eglantine, my dear—shouldn't you wait till you see them? You've no idea how well the Mitchells get on.

MADAME FRABELLE: I've no doubt of it. And of course I don't

know that he—Mr. Mitchell, I mean—even realizes what you are to him. But *I* do!

EDITH: Wait till you see them.

MADAME FRABELLE: From what your husband says I gather you see them often.

EDITH: Very often.

MADAME FRABELLE: He and Bruce are together at the Foreign Office. And I know Bruce greatly admires him. But now and then I sense a tinge of bitterness in the way he speaks. The other day he was describing their fancy-dress ball; and really, Edith, his description of Mr. Mitchell's costume would have been almost spiteful in any other man!

EDITH: Well, my dear—but Mr. Mitchell *is* over sixty. And he *was* got up as a black poodle!

MADAME FRABELLE: But he's a fine-looking man, isn't he? And very pleasant, and very hospitable?

EDITH: Oh, yes—of course.

MADAME FRABELLE: On your birthday last week that magnificent basket of flowers came from Mr. Mitchell, didn't it?

EDITH: From *both* the Mitchells, my dear…. But really, Eglantine, I think you'll be a little bit disappointed if you think Mr. Mitchell's at all the romantic type.

MADAME FRABELLE: Oh, I don't think *that!* But something tells me there's a strange attraction.

EDITH: A strange attraction….

MADAME FRABELLE: I never saw a more perfect wife than you, my dear—nor a more perfect mother. But these things should be nipped in the bud—*nipped in the bud!* They get hold of you sometimes before you know where you are. (*With relish, drawing nearer*) And think how terrible it would be to break up *two* homes!

EDITH: Oh, really, Eglantine—I must stop you there! You don't think of elopements, surely!

MADAME FRABELLE: Not *necessarily.* But, dear Edith, I've seen a great deal in my time. And the very households—*ménages,* as we say abroad—the very households that seem most calm and peaceful sometimes—*sometimes*— (*Again with relish*) Wouldn't it be dreadful to live a double life!

EDITH: Eglantine, you don't imagine there's an intrigue going on between me and Mr. Mitchell!

MADAME FRABELLE: No, no, no—not now—not *yet*. But you don't quite know, my dear Edith, how one can be carried away.

EDITH: Carried away?

MADAME FRABELLE: As I was sitting upstairs thinking—

EDITH: You think too much, my dear.

MADAME FRABELLE: It came to me like this. *I* mean to be the one to put things right. My dear child, a woman of the world like me *sees* things. You two ought to be blissfully happy. You're made for each other—I mean you and Bruce.

EDITH: Do you really think so?

MADAME FRABELLE: Absolutely! But this—what shall I say?—this *fascination* is coming between you. At first, no doubt, at the stage you're now in, it seems all romance, all excitement. But later on— Now, Edith, dear, promise me you won't be angry for what I've said. You don't think I'm a horrid, interfering old thing, do you?

EDITH: Indeed I *don't!* You're a dear!

MADAME FRABELLE: Well, we won't speak of it any more—till after Tuesday. And meanwhile take my advice, my dear. Throw yourself into other things!

EDITH: Other things?

MADAME FRABELLE: Why don't you refurnish your boudoir?

EDITH: I rather like my room, you know.

MADAME FRABELLE: And so do I. It's charming. But a change, dear—a change of *entourage,* as we say abroad—would do you good.

EDITH: Well, we must really think that out.

MADAME FRABELLE: And you're not cross?

EDITH: Cross? I don't know when I've enjoyed a conversation half so much! (*Her voice trails off as they go out arm-in-arm.*)

CURTAIN

Scene Two

Morning. EDITH *and* BRUCE *are seated on the sofa reading newspapers.*

EDITH (*putting down her newspaper*): Fancy, Bruce. Yesterday morning—in Fortnum's—guess who I met?

BRUCE (*absently, from behind his newspaper*): I really couldn't guess, Edith.

EDITH: I met Teddy Ross—Aylmer's son. (BRUCE *is silent.*) *You* know—Aylmer Ross.

BRUCE (*absently*): Oh, really—Aylmer Ross. (*Suddenly comprehending, putting down his newspaper*) What! Did you say Aylmer Ross?

EDITH: Aylmer's been wounded at the front. They've taken their old house again—in Jermyn Street. Aylmer's being brought home today.

BRUCE: Today!

EDITH: Teddy's to meet him at Charing Cross this afternoon.

BRUCE: Was the wound serious?

EDITH: They were anxious at first, but he's already much improved.

BRUCE: Capital chap, Aylmer. I always liked him.

EDITH: Among other things his leg was broken, and he still walks with a cane.

BRUCE (*fretfully*): Well, Edith, I really can't help it. *I'd* be at the front if it weren't for my neurotic heart. Still, it might have been just as well to die for my country, and get some glory, as to die of heart trouble here.

EDITH: Oh, Bruce—you look the picture of health!

BRUCE (*admiring himself in the glass*): I do have a bit of sunburn, don't I? Funny how I do catch the sun. I asked Dr. Braithwaite about it the other day.

EDITH (*smiling*): Really? You consulted Dr. Braithwaite about your sunburn?

BRUCE: What are you smiling at? He said it's caused by the extreme delicacy of the mucous membrane.

EDITH: Well, my dear boy, you needn't worry—it's very becoming. (*She takes up a letter.*) Oh, here's a letter from Lady Conroy.

BRUCE (*interested*): Lady Conroy!

EDITH (*reading*): "My dear Mrs. Ottley, Do excuse my troubling you, but could you give me a little information? Someone has asked me about Madame Frabelle. I know she is a friend of yours, and is staying with you, and I said so; also I fancy it is due to you that I have the pleasure of knowing her anyhow.

"Could you tell me who she was before she married? What her husband was, and anything else about her? That she is most charming and clever I know, of course. To say she is a friend of yours is enough to say that. But the rest I forget.

"I remain, yours most sincerely, Kathleen Conroy."

(EDITH *hands the letter to* BRUCE.)

BRUCE (*reading*): "P.S. Remember me to Madame Frabelle." (*He returns the letter to* EDITH.)

EDITH (*laughing*): Isn't this too delightful! She sends Madame Frabelle to me with a letter of introduction—and then she asks me who she is!

BRUCE: Well, Lady Conroy is a most charming person. You must give her all the information she wants.

EDITH: But all I know I only know from *her!*

BRUCE: Then tell her what she told *you*. Madame Frabelle told us candidly she made her acquaintance at the hotel. But it's absurd to tell Lady Conroy *that*.

(EDITH *goes to the writing table, sits down, and begins writing a letter.*)

EDITH (*speaking as she writes*): "My dear Lady Conroy, I understand Madame Frabelle is a clever woman who wishes to study English life in her native land. She is of good family; she was a Miss Eglantine Pollard, and is the widow of a well-to-do French wine merchant. I believe Madame Frabelle has several friends and connections in London."

BRUCE: The Mitchells, for instance.

EDITH: Oh, yes—that's a good idea. (*Writing*) "She knows the Mitchells very well. I think you know them also; they are very great friends of ours. Mr. Mitchell is in the Foreign Office."

BRUCE: And the Cannons? And Lord and Lady Selsey?

EDITH: Yes. (*Writing*) "She has other friends in London, I believe, but she has not troubled to look them up. The more one sees of her the better one likes her. She is most charming and amiable, and makes friends wherever she goes. Yours very sincerely, Edith Ottley." (*She seals the letter.*)

BRUCE: Edith, dear—you know that peculiar feeling I sometimes have?

EDITH: Which, dear?

BRUCE: You know that sort of emptiness in the feet, and heaviness in the head, and twitching of the eyelids that I get?

EDITH: Yes?

BRUCE: Well, Madame Frabelle has given me a complete cure. It seems her husband (by the way, *what* a brute *he* must have been, and *what* a life *that* poor woman led!)—it seems her husband had something of the same kind.

EDITH: Which, dear?

BRUCE: How do you mean—"Which"? Which what?

EDITH: Which peculiar feeling?

BRUCE: What peculiar feeling are we talking about?

EDITH: I said, which peculiar feeling did Monsieur Frabelle have?

BRUCE (*suspicious*): What are you trying to get at, Edith?

EDITH: Was it the emptiness in the feet, or the heaviness in the head, or the twitching of the eyelids that Monsieur Frabelle suffered from?

BRUCE: It seems he had a little of all three. But what do you think he did?

EDITH: I haven't the slightest idea, Bruce.

BRUCE: He took tisane. Tisane. It's a simple remedy, but a very good thing.

EDITH: Did he bathe his eye with it?

BRUCE: Oh, my dear Edith, you must be wool-gathering! He drank it—that's what he did, and that's what *I'm* going to do. Eglantine—uh—Madame Frabelle would go straight to the kitchen and show you how to make it if you like.

EDITH: *I* don't mind—if Cook doesn't.

BRUCE: Then there's another thing Madame Frabelle suggested.

EDITH: Another thing?

BRUCE: She thinks it would do me a world of good to spend a day in the country.

EDITH: Oh, really? A day in the country. What a good idea!

BRUCE: Perhaps a day on the river. She's not been there for years.

EDITH: Splendid!

BRUCE (*trying to conceal his eagerness*): Well, how about next Saturday?

EDITH: Next Saturday, by all means. What time shall we start? (*Suddenly remembering*) Only—oh, dear! I promised to take Archie to an afternoon performance next Saturday.

BRUCE (*brightening up*): Did you, though? Rather hard on poor Archie to disappoint him. Mind you, Edith—I don't believe in *spoiling* children. But on the other hand I don't think it's good to disappoint them quite so much as *that*. And after all—well, a promise to a *child!*

EDITH: It does seem rather a shame.

BRUCE: Well, then, look here, Edith. Suppose we do it—suppose *you* do it, I mean. Suppose you go with Archie. He's to lunch with my mother, isn't he?

EDITH: Yes, dear. But we were to have fetched him from there and taken him on to the theatre.

BRUCE: Well, then, *do it,* my dear girl! *Do it!* Stick to your plan!

Don't let *me* spoil your afternoon! Gracious heaven! *I* can take care of Madame Frabelle.

EDITH: Of course, Bruce.

BRUCE: So that's settled, then. *I'll* take her on the river. I don't mind in the least. I'm only too pleased—delighted!

EDITH: Bruce, dear—

BRUCE: Oh, don't thank me, dear girl! I know one ought to exert oneself for a guest—especially a widow… here in England… during the war. Hang it, it's the least one can do! (*He sees* MADAME FRABELLE *at the door.*) Ah, Madame Frabelle! Good morning!

MADAME FRABELLE (*all smiles*): Good morning, Mr. Ottley! Good morning, my dear Edith!

BRUCE: Madame Frabelle, Edith and I have been talking. I'll be happy to take you on the river on Saturday while Edith takes Archie to the theatre.

MADAME FRABELLE (*delighted*): Oh, Mr. Ottley—I *dote* on the river!

BRUCE: What part of the river do you like?

MADAME FRABELLE: Oh, any part. Don't ask *me!* Anything you suggest is sure to be right.

BRUCE: How about Maidenhead?

MADAME FRABELLE: Maidenhead…. Maidenhead….You know far more about these things than I do, Mr. Ottley. But isn't Maidenhead just a wee bit—commonplace? I mean—a little noisy, a little crowded.

BRUCE: By Jove, yes—you're quite right! Madame Frabelle's perfectly right, Edith…. Well, what about Shepperton?

MADAME FRABELLE: Shepperton. Oh, lovely! Dear little town. But Shepperton isn't exactly what *I* call the *river,* if you know what I mean.

BRUCE: Well, could *you* suggest a place?

MADAME FRABELLE: Oh, I'm the worst person in the world to suggest anything. And I know so little of the river. But how about Kingston?

BRUCE: Kingston. That would be charming.

MADAME FRABELLE: Kyngestown, as it used to be called—in the days when Saxon kings were crowned there. Wasn't it Kingston? Didn't great Caesar cross the river at Kingston? Didn't the Roman legions camp on the sloping uplands?

BRUCE (*gasping*): Madame Frabelle—you know everything!

MADAME FRABELLE: Oh, no, Mr. Ottley—I don't know *every-thing*. But I *do* remember a *little*—just a *little*—about *history*. Ah—poor, weak King Edwy!

BRUCE (*shaking his head*): Yes, indeed. Poor chap!

MADAME FRABELLE: *How* he must have hated that place!

BRUCE: Rather!

EDITH (*to* MADAME FRABELLE): But *you* won't hate it, my dear. *You* won't hate it at all. (*She goes out.*)

MADAME FRABELLE: But, Mr. Ottley—will *you* do the rowing—I mean Saturday on the river?

BRUCE: Of course—of course.

MADAME FRABELLE: How athletic you are, Mr. Ottley!

BRUCE: If I'd stuck to it, you know, I'd have done well in the rowing line. At one time I thought of going in for Henley—the regatta, you know. But with that beastly Foreign Office one can't keep up anything of *that* sort.

MADAME FRABELLE: No—I suppose not.

BRUCE: But my muscle *is* fairly good, you know. (*He extends his arm, hitting it hard.*) Not bad—eh?—for a London man who never has any practice.

MADAME FRABELLE (*all admiration*): No, *indeed!*

BRUCE: A few years ago my arm was seventeen inches round just below the elbow.

MADAME FRABELLE: Seventeen inches! Just fancy!

BRUCE: So on Saturday I'll be happy to row.

MADAME FRABELLE: And if you like, I'll be happy to relieve you.

BRUCE: How do you mean—relieve me?

MADAME FRABELLE: I mean *I'll* row—I'll sit in the stern—row!

BRUCE: Perhaps you've forgotten the names of the different parts of a boat, Madame Frabelle.

MADAME FRABELLE: Oh, I think not, Mr. Ottley. It's a good while since I was on the river, but it's not the sort of thing one easily forgets, and I'm supposed to have *rather* a good memory. (*She sits down on the sofa.*)

BRUCE: I'm sure you have a wonderful memory, Madame Frabelle. Still, where you sit to row is *not* the stern.

MADAME FRABELLE (*quickly changing the subject*): Oh, I do admire the scenery on the river! I love those distant glimpses of the grey old palace of the Tudors. Can you imagine what it was like when it was gay all day with the clanking of steel and the prancing of horses! And think of the evenings in that wonderful old palace with its panelled walls, and its cold stone corridors, and the echo of feet that are no longer there!

BRUCE: Echo of feet that are no longer there? But how could that be?

MADAME FRABELLE: I mean the *imaginary* echo.

BRUCE: Imaginary—ah, yes! You're very imaginative, aren't you, Madame Frabelle? Well, I don't know whether it's imagination or not, but do you know, I fancy that peculiar feeling of mine seems to be coming on again. (*He sits down beside her on the sofa.*)

MADAME FRABELLE: What peculiar feeling?

BRUCE: I told you about it the other night. A sort of emptiness in the feet, and heaviness in the head, and twitching of the eyelids.

MADAME FRABELLE: It's nearly eleven o'clock in the morning, Mr. Ottley. Perhaps you're hungry.

BRUCE: It may be. I had no breakfast.

MADAME FRABELLE: Nor did I.

BRUCE: Well, don't you feel you'd like some coffee?

MADAME FRABELLE: Oh, no—oh, dear, no! Still, I daresay some food would do *you* good, Mr. Ottley—keep you up.

BRUCE: But you must have something too.

MADAME FRABELLE: Oh, must I? Oh, very well—just to keep you company…. Oh, how I should like to go over Hampton Court!

BRUCE: Shall we take a guide?

MADAME FRABELLE: Certainly *not! I* know more about Hampton Court than any guide does! Oh, to think of King Charles II's lovely, languid ladies—how charming they were!

BRUCE: They wore very low dresses.

MADAME FRABELLE (*looking away modestly*): And how exquisite the garden is!

BRUCE: Yes—isn't it!

MADAME FRABELLE: There's nothing like England, I always say.

BRUCE: How exactly our tastes agree!

MADAME FRABELLE: Oh, do they? (*Her hand reaches the edge of the sofa. Somehow* BRUCE*'s hand reaches over it.*)

BRUCE: What small hands you have!

MADAME FRABELLE: Oh, no! I take sixes.

BRUCE (*examining her hand*): I suppose these rings have—uh—associations for you, Madame Frabelle?

MADAME FRABELLE (*sighing, shaking her head*): This one—yes, this one—the sapphire recalls old memories.

BRUCE (*with a tinge of bitterness*): A present from your husband, I suppose?

MADAME FRABELLE (*sighing*): Ah! Memories! Memories!

(BENNETT *enters.* BRUCE *and* MADAME FRABELLE *quickly draw apart and rise from the sofa.*)

BENNETT (*announcing*): Sir Tito Landi!

(SIR TITO LANDI *enters. He is a small, thin, slight man aged sixty. With his white moustache, pink and white complexion, and large blue eyes, his dandified dress, his eyeglass and buttonhole, he has the fresh fair look of an Englishman, the dry brilliance of a Parisian, and the diabolic humour of a Neapolitan. He speaks English with a charming continental accent; he speaks French with a perfect Parisian accent.* BENNETT *goes out.*)

BRUCE (*coming forward*): Ah, Sir Tito! Here you are!

LANDI (*proffering his hand*): Bruce.

BRUCE: Do you know Madame Frabelle? (*Introducing*) Sir Tito Landi.

LANDI (*bowing ceremoniously*): Madame Frabelle. How do you do.

MADAME FRABELLE (*eagerly*): Oh, Sir Tito—how thrilling to meet you at last! I've been longing to have a talk!

LANDI: A talk? With *me?*

MADAME FRABELLE: About the arts. Oh, I *dote* on the arts! And I understand you're quite modern in your views!

LANDI (*horrified*): I? Modern? Really, Madame Frabelle, you're quite mistaken. I don't think I'm modern at all.

MADAME FRABELLE: Oh, I'm so glad! I've such a worship myself for tradition! I'm so thankful you have too.

LANDI: But, Madame Frabelle—I don't know that I have.

MADAME FRABELLE: It's true, then, what I heard—I felt it the moment we met—I mean, you're a—you're a—Bohemian!

LANDI (*horrified*): A *what?* Good heavens, madame, do you know who I am?

BRUCE: Sir Tito is a musician. He composes songs.

MADAME FRABELLE: Oh, I knew it all the time! I could *feel* it! *How* charming! How *very* charming!

(EDITH *enters.*)

EDITH: Did someone ring? (*Seeing* LANDI) Oh, Landi!

LANDI: Edith, *ma chère.* (*He kisses* EDITH *affectionately on the cheek.*)

EDITH: How good to see you!

MADAME FRABELLE (*silenced*): Well, Edith, *if* you will excuse me—

EDITH: Certainly, my dear.

MADAME FRABELLE (*coldly*): Good morning, Sir Tito.

LANDI (*bowing ceremoniously*): Madame Frabelle.

(MADAME FRABELLE *goes out.*)

BRUCE (*cordially*): Good morning, Sir Tito.

LANDI (*smiling*): Bruce.

(BRUCE *goes out.* LANDI *immediately relaxes.*)

EDITH: Well, what do you think of her?

LANDI: Madame Frabelle? *C'est une bonne vieille. Bonne, mais bête!*

EDITH (*amused*): Really!

LANDI (*laughing*): *Bête comme ses pieds, ma chère! Tiens, ma chère Edith, tu ne vois pas quelque chose?*

EDITH: What?

LANDI: *La Mère Frabelle. Elle est folle de ton mari!*

EDITH: Oh, really, Landi! That's your fancy!

LANDI: *Farncy! Farncy! Je me suis monté l'imagination, peut-être! J'ai un rien de fièvre, sans doute! C'est une idée que j'ai, comme ça. Eh bien! Non! Nous verrons. Je te dis qu'elle est amoureuse de Bruce.*

EDITH: He's very devoted to *her,* I know. And I daresay he's a little in love with her—in a way. But she—

LANDI (*laughing*): *C'est tout le contraire! Lui, c'est moins; il est flatté. Il la trouve une femme intelligente. Mais elle! Tu es folle de ne pas voir ça, Edith. Enfin! Si ça l'amuse?*

EDITH: Madame Frabelle has got it into her head that Mr. Mitchell and I are attached to each other.

LANDI: *Naturellement. Elle veut s'excuser—la pauvre.*

EDITH: But she really believes it!

LANDI: *Elle voit double, alors!* (*Suddenly serious*) But, Edith, my dear—it mustn't happen again. It simply mustn't.

EDITH: What mustn't happen again?

LANDI: My dear child, don't spoil Bruce. Don't let him think he can always be running away and coming back.

EDITH: No—*that* must never happen again.

LANDI: You really like Madame Frabelle so much, my dear?

EDITH: Really I do. The more I know her the better I like her.

LANDI: And she keeps Bruce in good temper?

EDITH: Well, why shouldn't she? (*Laughing*) I'm not afraid of Madame Frabelle. After all, Bruce may be thirty-seven, but *she's* fifty.

LANDI: You know my old-fashioned ideas, Edith. I never approve of a third person living with a married couple.

EDITH: Oh—*living!* She's only been with us a month.

LANDI: But you don't think she's going away before the end of the season?

EDITH: Well, she can't easily settle down just now, on account of the war. She's never had a house of her own since her husband died.

LANDI: I see.

EDITH: But, Landi, dearest—I've been awfully anxious—

LANDI: Anxious, my dear? *Qu'est-ce qu'il y a?*

EDITH: I've just heard some bad news. Aylmer Ross has been wounded at the front.

LANDI: Aylmer Ross!

EDITH: He's being brought home to London today.

LANDI: *Du calme, mon enfant. Du calme!*

EDITH: But I *am* anxious, Landi.

LANDI: *Ça se voit!*

EDITH: Do you think—?

LANDI: *Ce ne sera rien.* It's the best thing that could happen. I suppose you want to see him, Edith?

EDITH: He may not want to see *me.*

LANDI: Oh, yes, he will! You were the first person he thought of…. Well, my dear, I'll go and see him tomorrow, and I'll let you know every detail.

EDITH: Oh, thank you, Landi, dear! But even if he wishes to see me, ought I to go?

LANDI: That I don't know. But *you* will…. Good-bye, my child. (*He kisses her on the cheek.*)

EDITH: Good-bye, Landi. (*She accompanies him to the door.*) And thank you, my dear. (LANDI *goes out. The door slams and* EDITH *returns. She goes to the writing table to pick up a book; she is about to leave the room when she sees* MADAME FRABELLE *passing in the hall.*) Oh, Eglantine! You remember, don't you, we're lunching with the Mitchells today.

MADAME FRABELLE: Oh, yes, my dear. Of course I remember! What a pity your husband can't come! (*Archly, shaking her finger at* EDITH) Ah, you naughty girl! I don't believe you really think so!

EDITH: Eglantine, have you seriously talked yourself into thinking Mr. Mitchell is anything to me?

MADAME FRABELLE: I don't say you're in *love* with him, Edith. But his devotion to you anyone with half an eye can see. And some day—some day your interest in him may take you by surprise!

EDITH: It's *your* interest in him that surprises *me*. He's a good friend, and we like him very much. But for anything else—

MADAME FRABELLE: It's really rather wonderful, Edith, dear, you've never had a thought beyond your husband—even the merest dream. It's really rather wonderful it's never occurred to you that anyone else might have suited your temperament better.

EDITH: Really?

MADAME FRABELLE: It isn't everyone, my dear, who'd appreciate your husband as *you* do. To *me*, of course, he's a very charming man. He inspires in me a feeling almost of—of *motherly* interest. (*Laughing*) I even feel sometimes as if I'd like to take care of him myself!

EDITH: Really!

MADAME FRABELLE: It wouldn't have been a bad thing for Bruce to have married a woman a little older than himself. But you, Edith—you're so young. You were a mere girl when you married him, and I could imagine some of his ways might irritate a very young woman. I suppose Bruce was quite handsome?

EDITH: Oh, yes—quite handsome. But then he still is.

MADAME FRABELLE: As I told you before, Edith—though I think you're an ideal wife, you don't give me the impression of being in love with him…. I hope you don't take this as an impertinence, my dear?

EDITH: Oh, no—not at all! For that matter I'm not sure I *am* an ideal wife.

MADAME FRABELLE: Your mother-in-law told me the other day you'd been a perfect wife. She said you'd even made sacrifices. (*Confidentially*) Edith, my dear—you've never had anything to forgive, surely?

EDITH (*a bit too quickly*): Oh, no—never.

MADAME FRABELLE: She said Bruce had been occasionally attracted—only very slightly, of course—to other women.

EDITH: Really?

MADAME FRABELLE: But she said you were the only person he *really* cares for.

EDITH: Oh, I doubt if Bruce ever thinks much of anyone else…. But come, my dear—we must change for lunch.

(*They go out together.*)

CURTAIN

Scene Three

Afternoon. EDITH *and* BRUCE *are seated on the sofa having tea.*

EDITH (*laughing*): Oh, Bruce! Another letter from Lady Conroy!

BRUCE: Lady Conroy!

EDITH: Listen to this. (*Reading*) "My dear Edith, Thank you so much for your nice letter. I remember now, of course—Madame Frabelle was a friend of the Mitchells, whom I know so well and like so much. She has other friends in London, but she has not troubled to look them up. She was a Miss Pollard, you know—a very good family. And as I always understood, the more one sees of her the better one likes her. Ever yours, Kathleen Conroy." (*She hands the letter to* BRUCE.)

BRUCE (*reading*): "P.S. Madame Frabelle's husband was a well-to-do French wine merchant, and I believe a very charming man." (*He returns the letter to* EDITH.)

EDITH (*laughing*): One of these days I'll write and ask Lady Conroy who Madame Frabelle is. And she'll answer that Madame Frabelle is a great friend of the Ottleys and the Mitchells.

BRUCE: Well—now we've taken all the responsibility on ourselves.

EDITH: I really don't mind. There's obviously no harm in Madame Frabelle.

BRUCE: She's a very clever woman. I'm always interested in what she has to say. And I don't mind telling you, Edith, I'm nearly always guided by it.

EDITH: So am I. She's so invariably wrong she's really quite a useful guide. I'm never quite sure of my own judgement until Madame Frabelle has contradicted it…. Oh, by the way, Bruce— she's promised to dine with the Mitchells tomorrow night.

BRUCE (*suddenly incensed*): Dine with the Mitchells! Tomorrow night! Well, *really!* Upon my word! This is a bit *too* much!

EDITH: Why, Bruce!

BRUCE: It's quite a shock, isn't it, when you find old friends throwing you over like this.

EDITH: Bruce, dear—

BRUCE: I've never been so surprised in all my life!

EDITH: I don't see anything so strange about it, Bruce. It's natural enough they should've asked her.

BRUCE: Oh, it is, is it? How would they ever have known her but for us?

EDITH: How could they ask her without knowing her? Besides, we went there last. We lunched with them on Tuesday.

BRUCE: That's not the point, Edith. You miss the point entirely. Unfortunately you always do. You have a woman's weakness, my dear. You're incapable of arguing logically.

EDITH: Bruce—

BRUCE: *I* consider it a downright insult—perhaps *injury* is the proper word—to take away our guest and not ask us.

EDITH: Bruce—

BRUCE: Not that I should've gone. I shouldn't have dreamt of going in any case. Besides, we're engaged to dine with my mother.

EDITH: Mrs. Mitchell knew that. That's why she asked Madame Frabelle—because she'd be alone.

BRUCE: Oh, how like you, Edith! Always take the other side!... But perhaps it's for the best. The truth is, I'm getting a bit tired of the Mitchells. If they'd pressed me ever so much, nothing in the world would've made me break my promise to my mother.

EDITH: Well, then, it's all right. So why complain?

(BENNETT *enters bringing a letter on a salver.*)

BENNETT: A letter, ma'am—just delivered by hand.

EDITH: Oh, thank you, Bennett. (*She takes the letter;* BENNETT *goes out.*) It's from the Mitchells! (*She opens the letter and reads.*) They ask if you and I can't manage to come to dinner all the same, if we aren't afraid of offending your mother. They say we can go to Mrs. Ottley's at any time, and they particularly want us to meet some people tomorrow night—a small party, unexpectedly got up. (*She goes to the telephone.*) Of course you won't go.

BRUCE: Won't *go!*

EDITH: You said you wouldn't go under any circumstances.

BRUCE: Look here, Edith—

EDITH: I'll refuse, shall I?

BRUCE: Certainly *not!* Of *course* I'll go! It *is* perfectly true we can go to my mother's at any time. Besides, I don't think it's quite fair to old friends like the Mitchells to throw them over when they ask us to do them this special favour.

EDITH: You don't think, perhaps, someone has disappointed them, and they're asking us at the last minute to fill up?

BRUCE: Certainly *not!* The idea of such a thing! As if they'd treat *me* like that!

EDITH: All right, Bruce. Just as you wish. But your mother will be disappointed. (MADAME FRABELLE *enters.*) Ah, Eglantine! Do come in. We're just having tea.

MADAME FRABELLE: Oh, thank you, my dear. I'm frightfully busy this afternoon, but I think I *can* spare time for one small cup…. Oh, good afternoon, Mr. Ottley!

BRUCE (*eagerly*): Good afternoon, Madame Frabelle!

(EDITH *pours a cup of tea;* BRUCE *hands it to* MADAME FRABELLE.)

EDITH: We've just had a letter from Lady Conroy.

MADAME FRABELLE: Ah, dear Kathleen! I hope she's well.

BRUCE (*taking up a book*): Good heavens, Edith! You've dog-eared my book!

EDITH: Why, Bruce—I've only turned down a page!

BRUCE: You've dog-eared it, Edith! You've— It's really quite irritating, dear, how you take no notice of my rebukes.

EDITH: Why, Bruce!

BRUCE: What I say to you seems to go in one ear and out the other—just like water on a duck's back.

EDITH (*enjoying her jest*): How does the water on a duck's back get into the dog's ear—I mean the duck's ear?

BRUCE: Don't quibble with me, Edith!

EDITH: I'm sorry, Bruce. I'm truly sorry. I won't do it again.

BRUCE (*mimicking* EDITH): "Won't do it again"! Upon my word, Edith! *Upon my word!* (*He storms out of the room.*)

MADAME FRABELLE (*shaking her head*): Poor Edith! Poor Edith! What *shall* we do with our husbands?

EDITH: Well, I suppose they have their faults.

MADAME FRABELLE: Oh, men are all alike.

EDITH: Only *some* men. Besides, to a woman—I mean, a *nice* woman—there's no such thing as men. There's a *man*. And either she's so fond of him she can talk of nothing else, or so much in love with him she never mentions his name.

MADAME FRABELLE: Men often say *women* are all alike.

EDITH: When a man says that, he means there's only one woman in the world, and he's in love with her, and she's not in love with him.

MADAME FRABELLE: Men are not so faithful as women.

EDITH: Perhaps not. And yet I think a man is often more in love with the woman he's unfaithful *to* than with the woman he's unfaithful *with*.

(BENNETT *enters.*)

BENNETT (*announcing*): Mr. Aylmer Ross!

(AYLMER ROSS *enters, walking with a cane. He is forty-one, tall, handsome, gentlemanly.* BENNETT *goes out.*)

EDITH (*cordially*): Aylmer, my dear! *What* a nice surprise! (*They shake hands.*) Do you know Madame Frabelle?

MADAME FRABELLE (*eagerly*): Oh, how do you do, Mr. Ross! I feel I already know you—Edith has mentioned you so often, and always in such glowing terms.

EDITH: You're looking awfully well, Aylmer. Miss Clay must be a splendid nurse.

MADAME FRABELLE (*archly*): I *hear* she's quite charming! And wonderfully pretty too!

AYLMER (*turning to* MADAME FRABELLE): She's a good nurse. She's been awfully kind. But she's leaving soon.

MADAME FRABELLE: Oh, Mr. Ross! I'm sure if *I* were a young man I should be very sorry when she had to leave *me!*

AYLMER: Possibly, Madame Fradelle. Possibly. But you're not a young man, are you? And neither am I.

MADAME FRABELLE (*silenced*): Well, Edith, *if* you will excuse me—

EDITH: Certainly, my dear.

MADAME FRABELLE (*coldly*): Good afternoon, Mr. Ross. (*She goes out.*)

EDITH: Oh, Aylmer—how good of you to come!

AYLMER: How good of you to *let* me come!

EDITH: Shall I pour your tea?

AYLMER: Yes. Let's get it over. (EDITH *laughs, pours a cup of tea, and hands it to* AYLMER.) What a jolly dress!

EDITH: Oh, I *am* glad you like it.

AYLMER: I love it. And I love *you.* (EDITH *smiles.*) Look here, Edith, have you forgotten me?

EDITH: You can see I haven't, or you wouldn't be here.

AYLMER: Don't fence with me, Edith. I mean, really. Are you the same as when I went away?

EDITH: Aylmer, do you think we'd better talk this way?

AYLMER: We *must. I* must. I can't endure the torture of seeing you just like anybody else. You know I told you—

EDITH: You told me you'd never be a mere friend. But everything's so different now!

AYLMER: Everything's *not* different. You're just the same, and so am I. Except that I care for you far more than I ever did.

EDITH: Oh, Aylmer! Do change your mind from what you said when you went away.

AYLMER: Do you wish to be friends, then?

EDITH: You know I do!

AYLMER: Then let's look at things as they are.... Edith, dear, as far as I make out, you're sacrificing yourself to Bruce. When he ran away with that girl—that Miss Townsend—and begged you to divorce him, you could've done it. Everything would've been right—even before the world.

EDITH: But it wasn't *for* the world, Aylmer. It was for *myself*. I felt Bruce needed me. I felt he'd go wrong without me.

AYLMER: Why should you care? Did he consider *you*?

EDITH: That isn't the point, dear boy. I felt as if he were my son, so to speak. I felt I had a sort of responsibility.

AYLMER: Responsibility! Rubbish! Quixotic rubbish!…Well, now—he *hasn't* run away. He's stayed with you for four years— utterly incapable of appreciating you, and at the same time bothering you to death.

EDITH: Oh, Aylmer!

AYLMER: You're frittering yourself away, Edith—and all for nothing.

EDITH: But Archie—

AYLMER: Don't you know I'd have looked after Archie better than he?

EDITH: But he *is* Archie's father. And Archie just *may* keep him straight.

AYLMER: Edith, darling—leave Bruce. Come away with me.

EDITH (*staring*): Aylmer!

AYLMER: In six weeks, when he's tired of telling his friends at the club about it, he'll make up his mind, I suppose, to divorce you. But do you suppose he'll keep Archie? Of course he won't!… Now, listen, Edith. Bruce will want to marry again, won't he?

EDITH: Very likely.

AYLMER: He's probably fascinated by that woman who's staying with you. What's her name? Madame Fradelle. Perhaps he's in love with her already.

EDITH: Quite possibly.

AYLMER: She's a very good sort. She's not a fool, like that Miss Townsend. She'd look after Bruce very well.

EDITH: So she would.

AYLMER: Bruce would adore her, be under her thumb, and

keep perfectly "straight," as you put it. And *you'd* get Archie, don't you see?

EDITH: Yes—with a bad reputation, and a cloud on my life!

AYLMER: My dear Edith, you're only thinking of what the *world* says. How could *you* ever hurt Archie?

EDITH: Aylmer—

AYLMER: Edith, darling, hear me out. Is this the only country? After the war, won't everything be different? Thank goodness, I'm well provided for. Leave your own income to Bruce if you like. You know I've ten thousand a year.

EDITH: That has nothing to do with it.

AYLMER: It has *everything* to do with it! I can afford to bring up Archie as well as Teddy. We can marry. And in a year or two no one will think any more about it.

EDITH: My dear boy, will you listen to me?

AYLMER: Go on, Edith. I'll always listen to you.

EDITH: You don't realize it, but you're not well.

AYLMER: How like a woman! As soon as I talk sense you say I'm not well. A broken leg doesn't affect the brain, remember.

EDITH: Aylmer, dear, you've been thinking this over till you've lost your sense of proportion.

AYLMER: My dear girl, I've just *gained* it! Of course, if you don't care for me, my suggestion is perfectly mad. Perhaps you regard our romance as a pretty little story to look back on.

EDITH: You know I don't.

AYLMER: If you care for me as I do for you, you'll do as I ask.

EDITH: I might care quite as much and yet not do it.

AYLMER: Don't you see, Edith, if you still love me, your present life is a long, slow sacrifice to convention, or—as you say—to a morbid sense of responsibility.

EDITH: Aylmer—

AYLMER: As you well know, *I've* never changed. After the operation, when they thought I was dying, I showed Dulcie Clay your photograph and asked her to send it back to you. I told her my greatest wish was to see you again.

EDITH: Has nothing occurred to you about Dulcie Clay?

AYLMER: Nothing—except that I'm getting rid of her as soon as possible.

EDITH: She's madly in love with you, Aylmer.

AYLMER: Really, Edith—how does *she* come in? You *are* perverse!

EDITH: I'm not perverse. I see things.

AYLMER: It's your imagination, Edith. But even if it's not, it isn't *my* business—and it isn't yours.

EDITH: I think it is—a little.

AYLMER: If you talk like that, I'll send her away at once.

EDITH: Oh, Aylmer! How ungrateful of you to say such a thing! She's been an angel.

AYLMER: I don't *want* an angel! I want *you!*

EDITH (*laughing*): *What* a compliment!

AYLMER: Now you're going to say, "Ought you to talk so much? What is your temperature?" Oh, women *are* irritating—even the nicest!

EDITH (*laughing*): I'm afraid I *was* going to say something like that.

AYLMER: Most women treat a wounded man as if he were a sick child. It's the greatest rot…. (*Jesting*) Perhaps we should talk of something else to divert my thoughts. Hasn't it been lovely weather lately!

EDITH: Oh, Aylmer!

AYLMER: Perhaps you'd like to know how soon the war will be over. Oddly enough, I really don't know!

EDITH: Are you going back when you've recovered?

AYLMER: Of course I'm going back! And I want to go back with your promise. (*Gently, a little conscience-stricken*) But, dear Edith, I don't want to rush you. Forgive me. When shall I see you again?

EDITH: Whenever you like. And I'll think over what you said.

AYLMER: What a funny little speech! Oh, you're a jolly girl!

EDITH: A jolly girl! I'm thirty-five years old, with a boy at school!

AYLMER: You think too much of the almanac. I'm forty-one, with a son at the front.

EDITH: How on earth did you get your commissions?

AYLMER: Teddy and I told lies. He said he was eighteen, and I said I was thirty-nine.

EDITH: I see.

AYLMER: Will you write to me, Edith?

EDITH: No, I'll come to see you.

AYLMER: Will you bring Bruce or Madame Fradelle?

EDITH: Neither.

AYLMER: Do leave Madame Fradelle at home.

EDITH: Even though you don't like her, Aylmer, you might pronounce her name right. She's a very clever woman.

AYLMER: She's an utter fool.

EDITH (*laughing*): Same thing, very often. Now, darling, you mustn't worry! You mustn't! (*Her voice trails off as they go out together.*)

CURTAIN

Act Two

Scene One

Morning. EDITH *and* BRUCE *are seated at a small breakfast table near the window.*

BRUCE: Edith, dear.

EDITH: Yes, Bruce?

BRUCE: I have here a letter from Aylmer—Aylmer Ross, you know—asking me *most* particularly to call on him.

EDITH: Oh, really?

BRUCE: He wants me to come this afternoon at half-past four. I'll certainly go. I shan't lose a minute. (*He pockets the letter.*)

EDITH: I'm afraid you'll have to lose a *few* minutes, Bruce. It's only nine o'clock.

BRUCE (*suddenly incensed*): Look here, Edith!

EDITH: Yes, Bruce?

BRUCE: For God's sake, Edith!

EDITH: Bruce! What do you mean?

BRUCE: What do I mean! You ask me what I mean! You may well ask me what I mean!

EDITH: Then what is it you don't approve of?

BRUCE: What you just said. About several minutes being lost before half-past four.

EDITH: Oh, Bruce, dear, I didn't mean any harm.

BRUCE: Harm! Harm! It isn't a question of actual harm. I didn't say you meant to injure me, or even to hurt my feelings. But it's a way of speaking—a tone—that I think extremely unbecoming from you to me. Do you follow me, Edith? From *you* to *me.*

EDITH: That's a dark saying, Bruce…. Well, whatever I said I take it back.

160

BRUCE (*mollified, but not wishing to show it at once*): You should think before you speak. Prevention is better than cure.

EDITH: Yes—and a stitch in time saves nine. And it's no good crying over spilt milk. And two heads are better than one.... But really, Bruce, I didn't mean it.

BRUCE: What didn't you mean?

EDITH: Good heavens, I really don't remember!

BRUCE: Look here, Edith. When an old friend—an old friend of yours and mine, next door to a brother—when a friend like that is wounded at the front, fighting for our country—and, mind you, he behaved with remarkable gallantry, for it wasn't really necessary for him to go, as he was beyond the age—well, when a friend does a thing like that, and comes back wounded, and writes with his own hand asking me to go and see him—well, I think it's the *least* I can do! I don't know what *you* think, but *I* think it's the right thing.

EDITH: My dear Bruce, who could doubt it?

BRUCE: Read the letter for yourself. (*He takes the letter from his pocket and hands it to* EDITH.) There—you see. "Dear Ottley," he says. (*He goes to* EDITH*'s side of the table and leans over her, reading the letter aloud to her as she reads it to herself.*) "Dear Ottley, If you could look in tomorrow about half-past four, I should be very glad to see you. Yours sincerely, Aylmer Ross." Fairly cordial, don't you think?

EDITH: Very cordial indeed.

BRUCE: Perhaps you think it cold. (*He takes the letter from her hand and reads it again to himself.*)

EDITH: I think it very nice.

BRUCE (*pocketing the letter*): I fear Aylmer's depressed. He thinks I'll cheer him up.

EDITH: And I'm sure you will.

BRUCE: *What* a splendid fellow!

EDITH: Is he really?

BRUCE: You don't appreciate him, Edith. In my opinion Aylmer Ross is a hero.

EDITH: I hope you'll find him better.

BRUCE: *He'll* say so, anyhow. He's a brave chap!

EDITH: Is he really?

BRUCE: Oh, Edith, you don't know a hero when you see one! (MADAME FRABELLE *enters.*)

EDITH: Ah—here's Madame Frabelle.

MADAME FRABELLE (*smiling amiably*): Good morning, Edith, dear! Good morning, Mr. Ottley! I'm afraid I'm a little late. (*She takes her place at the table.*)

BRUCE: Oh, dear, no—not at all! *Not at all!* Of course, if you'd been a minute later I shouldn't have had the pleasure of seeing you before I went to the office.

MADAME FRABELLE: Well, I think I'm generally fairly punctual. But Archie came to my room and asked me to settle a question for him.

EDITH: How dreadful of Archie to bother you so early!

MADAME FRABELLE: Oh, no—not at all! I assure you I enjoy it. And besides, a boy with Archie's musical talents is bound to have the artistic temperament. And of course we all know what *that* means!

EDITH: If he were really musical I should've thought he'd be more harmonious.

BRUCE: Oh, by the way, Edith, did you consult Landi?

EDITH: Landi can see no sign of musical genius *yet.*

BRUCE: Dear, dear!

MADAME FRABELLE: Oh, but I'm convinced he's wrong! I'm not at all sure, either, that a composer like Landi is necessarily the right person to judge of youthful genius.

EDITH: And yet you'd think, wouldn't you, he'd know a *bit* about it. I mean—they wouldn't have made him a baronet, would they, if he didn't understand his profession.

MADAME FRABELLE: Not at all! It doesn't follow. I mean—it doesn't follow that he's right about Archie. Did he try the boy's voice?

EDITH: He did.

MADAME FRABELLE: How?

EDITH: Well, he asked Archie to sing a few notes.

MADAME FRABELLE: And did he?

EDITH: He did. But they weren't the notes Landi asked him to sing.

MADAME FRABELLE: Oh!

EDITH: Then Landi played him two tunes, and found he didn't know one from the other.

MADAME FRABELLE: Well, what of that?

EDITH: Nothing at all—except that it showed Archie had no ear, as well as no voice.

MADAME FRABELLE: Ah—well! You just wait!

EDITH: Certainly I shall.

BRUCE (*rising from the table*): Oh, by the way, Madame Frabelle—I may be a little late for dinner tonight. I'm going to see an old friend who's been wounded in the war.

MADAME FRABELLE: Oh, really?

BRUCE: Mr. Aylmer Ross.

MADAME FRABELLE: How splendid!

BRUCE: Good-bye, Edith. (*He kisses* EDITH *perfunctorily on the cheek.*)

EDITH: Good-bye, dear. (*She rises and follows* BRUCE *to the door.*)

BRUCE: Good-bye, Madame Frabelle.

MADAME FRABELLE: Good-bye, Mr. Ottley. (BRUCE *goes out.*) Well, Edith! I thoroughly understand your husband's hero-worship for that man.

EDITH: Aylmer Ross? Oh, do tell me what you think of him!

MADAME FRABELLE: Edith, dear, I'm sorry to say it, but he's a hard, cold, cruel man.

EDITH: Really!

MADAME FRABELLE: Mr. Ross doesn't know what it is to feel emotion or sentiment or tenderness. He's incapable of passion of any kind. (EDITH *smiles.*) I see you're amused at my being right again. The truth is, Edith, I never make a mistake. Isn't it extraordinary!

EDITH: Isn't it!

MADAME FRABELLE: Consider his physiognomy. His brows show a narrow mind. His mouth shows bitterness. And his eyes! His eyes give away his chief characteristic—the thing one misses most in his personality.

EDITH: And what is that?

MADAME FRABELLE: Can't you see?

EDITH: I don't think I can.

MADAME FRABELLE: He has no sense of humour!

EDITH: And what do you think of his nurse?

MADAME FRABELLE: His nurse?

EDITH: Dulcie Clay.

MADAME FRABELLE: Really, Edith, I think I'd rather not say.

EDITH: Oh?

MADAME FRABELLE: Well, I want to be perfectly fair.

EDITH: Of course!

MADAME FRABELLE: I always want to be fair.

EDITH: Of course!

MADAME FRABELLE: Well, she *is* extremely pretty—I grant you *that*. But frankly, Edith, I don't *quite* like to say *what* I think of Miss Clay.

EDITH: As bad as *that!* Oh, do tell me, Eglantine!

MADAME FRABELLE (*yielding at last, savouring her moment*): Well, as I say, she's very, very pretty—*and* very, very clever. But she's deep and scheming. It's a sly, treacherous face.

EDITH: Sly and treacherous! I don't see that!

MADAME FRABELLE: Ah, my dear—you don't see half as much as I do!

EDITH: I should've said she's particularly open and frank.

MADAME FRABELLE: Ah, my dear—but that's all put on! Someday you'll see I'm right! To tell the truth, Edith, she gives me a shiver down my spine. I believe that girl capable of anything. *Anything!* That dark skin with those pale blue eyes!

EDITH: But Eglantine—you can't have looked at her fine features and her white hands.

MADAME FRABELLE: *Why* is she so dark?

EDITH: There may have been Italian or Spanish blood in her family.

MADAME FRABELLE (*ominously*): There may *indeed!*

EDITH: But, dearest Eglantine, it's not a symptom of crime!

MADAME FRABELLE: Mark my words, Edith—she's a dangerous woman!

(BENNETT *enters.*)

BENNETT (*announcing*): Sir Tito Landi!

(LANDI *enters;* EDITH *comes forward to greet him;* BENNETT *goes out.*)

EDITH: Landi, darling! You *are* an early bird!

LANDI: Just passing, my dear. Just passing.

MADAME FRABELLE: Dear Sir Tito! *What* a pleasure to see you again!

LANDI (*bowing ceremoniously*): Madame Frabelle.

MADAME FRABELLE: Your lovely songs have been ringing in my ears ever since I heard them!

LANDI: And where did you hear them, madame? On a piano-organ?

MADAME FRABELLE (*flirtatiously*): Oh, Sir Tito—you *are* wicked! Edith, dear, isn't he naughty! (*To* LANDI) I heard you when you sang here last.

LANDI: Ah—yes.

MADAME FRABELLE: Well, Edith—*if* you will excuse me—

EDITH: Certainly, my dear.

MADAME FRABELLE: Good morning, Sir Tito.

LANDI (*bowing ceremoniously*): Madame Frabelle. (MADAME FRABELLE *goes out.*) *Dieu merci! La vieille qui voit double! Elle me donne sur les nerfs ce matin.* (*Suddenly he puts his hand to his lips and blows a kiss toward the door.*)

EDITH (*laughing*): Who's *that* for?

LANDI: *C'est pour la vieille.*

EDITH: Madame Frabelle? Why do you kiss your hand to her?

LANDI: To keep her quiet. She thinks I'm so wicked she blushes and runs.

EDITH (*laughing*): Oh, Landi!

LANDI: I wonder whether she'll confess to you my passion for her, or whether she'll keep it to herself.

EDITH: I daresay she'll tell me. At least she'll ask if I think so or not.

LANDI: *Si elle te demande, tu diras que tu n'en sais rien!*

EDITH (*laughing*): Dearest Landi! Do sit down.

LANDI (*affectionately, peering at* EDITH *through his eyeglass*): *Cette enfant! Je l'ai vue en jupe courte, vous savez. Je l'ai vue naître! Elle a quelque chose, cette enfant. Oui, elle a quelque chose.* (*He sits down beside* EDITH.)

EDITH: Yes, Landi, there *is* something the matter. I want your advice.

LANDI: *Tout se sait; tout se fait; tout s'arrange.*

EDITH: Oh, it isn't one of *those* things, Landi!

LANDI: *Tiens! Tiens! Tiens!* How excited you are!

EDITH: You'll think I have reason to be excited when I tell you.

LANDI: *Eh bien, ma chère. Commence!*

EDITH: Aylmer Ross was here yesterday.

LANDI: Ah—Aylmer Ross.

EDITH: We had a long, long talk.

LANDI: Is everything the same?

EDITH: He says he cares for me now more than ever.

LANDI: And—?

EDITH: He wants me to leave Bruce and go away with him.

LANDI: To marry?

EDITH: Yes—to marry.

LANDI: And Archie?

EDITH: He wants to bring up Archie as his own son.

LANDI: And what did you say?

EDITH: I said I couldn't.

LANDI: And what did *he* say?

EDITH: He said I must.

LANDI: And how did he leave you?

EDITH: I told him I'd think over what he said.

LANDI: Well! (*A pause.*) Well, well! (*A pause.*) Edith, *ma chère,*
I think—

EDITH: What do you think?

LANDI: I think you must wait. You must wait and see. Really,
it's impossible, my dear child, for you to accept an elopement as
if it were a luncheon engagement. Besides, it's good for Aylmer
to be kept in doubt. Good for his health.

EDITH: His health?

LANDI: I mean the health of his love for you. You must vacil-
late, Edith. Sit on the fence. Offer the fence to him, but take it
away before he sits down. *Voilà!*

EDITH (*laughing*): But then this girl—Miss Clay. She's always
there.

LANDI: What's her nationality?

EDITH: How funny you should ask! I think she must be of
Spanish descent. She's so quiet, so religious, so very dark. And
yet such wonderful light blue eyes!

LANDI: *Quelle histoire! Qu'est-ce que ça fait?*

EDITH: The poor girl is mad about Aylmer.

LANDI: Spanish…. Does she wear a mantilla and use the cas-
tanets?

EDITH (*laughing*): Oh, Landi! How frivolous you are! Of course
not! She looks quite English!

LANDI: And yet you insist she's Spanish! Well, my advice is
this. If he has a secret alliance with Spain, you should assume
the Balkan attitude.

EDITH: Good gracious! What's that?

LANDI (*laughing*): *Farncy*—Mrs. Ottley doesn't know about
the Balkans!

EDITH (*laughing*): Oh, Landi!

LANDI (*suddenly serious*): Now, listen, *ma chère.* Don't see Aylmer
for a while.

EDITH: He wants me to go for a drive.

LANDI: Then go for a drive. But not this week. (*Shaking his head*) How Madame Frabelle loves Bruce!

EDITH: Really, Landi—occasionally you're as mistaken as she is. And *she* thinks I'm in love with Mr. Mitchell.

LANDI: That's because *elle voit double.*

EDITH: What makes you think—?

LANDI: I read between the lines, my dear—the lines on Madame Frabelle's face.

EDITH: But she hasn't any lines!

LANDI: Oh, go along, *ma chère.*

EDITH (*laughing*): Dearest Landi, I can't talk to you when you're so silly!

LANDI: There's no hurry, *ma chère.* Good heavens! The man's waited four years. He can wait another week.

EDITH: He's going back as soon as he's well. He wants me to promise before he goes.

LANDI: It's all right, Edith. We'll find a solution.

EDITH: But, dearest Landi—Aylmer's pressing me for an answer!

LANDI: He wants an elopement, I see. *Mais ça ne se fait pas!*

EDITH: Then what am I to say?

LANDI: *Rien. Rien.* And now I must go. Dear Edith, I promise to consider the question.

EDITH (*accompanying* LANDI *to the door*): Thank you, my darling. And before I see Aylmer again—

LANDI: Before you see Aylmer again, *ma chère,* you must see *me.*

EDITH: Dearest Landi!

(LANDI *kisses* EDITH *on the cheek and goes out.*)

CURTAIN

Scene Two

Afternoon. EDITH *is seated at the writing table, pen in hand.*

ARCHIE (*offstage, calling*): Mother! Oh, Mother! (*He runs in, much excited;* BENNETT *follows.*)

EDITH (*looking up from her writing*): Archie, dear, what is it?

ARCHIE: Oh, Mother, guess what! I've brought home a dog!

EDITH (*astonished*): A dog!

ARCHIE: Please, Mother, *do* let me keep it!

EDITH: Archie, darling—

ARCHIE: *Please,* Mother!

EDITH: What sort of dog is it?

ARCHIE: It isn't any particular *sort.* It's just a dog.

EDITH: But, my dear boy, you're going back to school tomorrow, and you can't take a dog with you.

ARCHIE: I'll teach Bennett to look after it.

EDITH (*laughing*): Bennett!

ARCHIE: It's an inconsistent dog.

EDITH: Inconsistent?

ARCHIE: Its face is like a terrier's, and its tail is like a spaniel's. But I think it might be trained to a bloodhound.

EDITH: And what use would a bloodhound be to Bennett?

ARCHIE: Well, you never know.

EDITH: Archie, darling, I'm afraid there isn't room in the house for a dog.

ARCHIE: Oh, Mother! We *must* keep it!

EDITH: Was it lost?

ARCHIE (*hesitating*): Well—not exactly.

EDITH: How did you find it?

ARCHIE: It was just walking along, and I took its chain. The chain was dragging on the ground.

EDITH (*shocked*): Archie! Did you steal it?

ARCHIE: Oh, no, Mother! I didn't steal— Its master had walked on. That's not stealing.

BENNETT: If Master Archie wants to keep a lot of dogs, ma'am, he'd better take 'em with him to school. I don't want nothin' to do with no dogs—not in this house! (*She goes out.*)

EDITH: There's only one thing to be done, Archie. You must take care of the dog tonight, and I'll advertise in the paper for its master.

ARCHIE (*protesting*): Oh, Mother!

EDITH: Don't you see, my dear, it isn't honest to keep it.

ARCHIE: But how can we advertise it? We don't even know its name!

EDITH: Well, it certainly won't be easy to describe!

ARCHIE: But it *will* be fun to see my name in the paper.

EDITH: Indeed you *won't* see your name in the paper!

ARCHIE (*sulking*): Well, I found it!

EDITH: Yes—but you had no right to find it, and still less to bring it home. I don't know what your father will say. Now, run along, Archie, darling. Mother's expecting Mr. Ross for tea.

ARCHIE: Mr. Aylmer Ross?

EDITH: Yes, dear.

(ARCHIE *starts to go, then turns.*)

ARCHIE (*considering*): Mother!

EDITH: Yes, darling?

ARCHIE: Why doesn't Father fight in the war?

EDITH: I told you before, darling. Your father's not very strong.

ARCHIE: Mother!

EDITH: Yes, dear?

ARCHIE: Is Aylmer older than Father?

EDITH: Aylmer's four years older.

ARCHIE: I wish I had a father who could fight—like Aylmer. And *I'd* like to fight too—like Teddy.

EDITH: Aylmer hasn't any wife and child to leave. And Teddy's eighteen; you're only ten.

ARCHIE: Mother!

EDITH: Yes, darling?

ARCHIE: But what's the *matter* with Father?

EDITH: Your father suffers from nerves.

ARCHIE: Nerves? What's nerves?

EDITH: Archie, dearest, I think it's time for your tea.

ARCHIE: Well—give my love to Aylmer.

EDITH: All right, dear.

ARCHIE: Mother!

EDITH: Yes, darling?

ARCHIE: I wish—I wish Aylmer was *my* father.

EDITH: Oh, Archie! You mustn't say that! You mustn't! Now, off to your tea!

(ARCHIE *goes out just as* BENNETT *enters.*)

BENNETT (*announcing*): Sir Tito Landi!

(LANDI *enters;* EDITH *comes forward to greet him;* BENNETT *goes out.*)

EDITH: Landi, dearest! How sweet of you to come!

LANDI: I got your message, Edith. I came at once. (*Checking his watch*) I've just a quarter of an hour.

EDITH: Oh, Landi, darling—since we last spoke I've completely changed!

LANDI: Completely changed?

EDITH: I'm in love with him all over again.

LANDI: In love with Aylmer Ross?

EDITH: I don't know how and I don't know why. When he first made the suggestion, it seemed wild. But the things he said—how absolutely true they are! Landi, my life's been wasted—utterly wasted. I've become so used to living this sort of half life I haven't even realized how much I cared for Aylmer.

LANDI: But you *were* quite content, my dear.

EDITH: Because I made myself so. Because I resolved to be satisfied. My life with Bruce was only a makeshift. Nothing but tact, tact, tact. I'm not deceiving myself now. I *am* in love with Aylmer.

LANDI: And Archie?

EDITH: With Aylmer there'd be no question of my ever leaving Archie.

LANDI: And Bruce?

EDITH: Oh, Bruce wouldn't mind. He'd be only too thankful for me to take Archie.

LANDI: And Aylmer?

EDITH: Oh, Aylmer's very well off. I'd never be a burden. I could leave *my* income to Bruce; he'd be quite independent. Oh, he'd take it. He'd find someone who'd look after him and make him quite happy…. You're shocked?

LANDI: *Ça ne m'étonne pas.*

EDITH: How wonderful of you to understand!

LANDI: But, Edith, I wonder—could you really go through with it?

EDITH: I believe I could now. You see, I mistook my own feelings. I thought I could live without love.

LANDI: I don't ask you to live without love. Why should a woman live without the very thing she was created for? But you know you hate publicity—vulgar scandal.

EDITH: Are you suggesting—?

LANDI: Many people have love in their lives *without* vulgar scandal.

EDITH: But I hate deceit, Landi. I couldn't lead a double life. And even if *I* could, *he* couldn't!

LANDI: *Pauvre garçon! Je l'admire.*

EDITH: Aylmer's not a man who could shake hands with Bruce and then deceive him.

LANDI: But, Edith, remember: before—even when Bruce ran away with another woman, you couldn't bear the thought of divorce.

EDITH: I know, I know. But I may have been wrong.

LANDI: Isn't this all rather sudden, my dear?

EDITH: Only because I've finally let myself go…. Oh, *do* encourage me, Landi! Suppose Aylmer goes out again and is killed, how miserable I'd feel to have disappointed him—for the second time!

LANDI: But suppose, as you say, he goes out again and is killed, and you *haven't* disappointed him…. And how is it your conscience regarding Bruce doesn't come into play now?

EDITH: Bruce doesn't seem to matter so much now.

LANDI: Because he isn't fighting?

EDITH: Oh, no—I never thought of that. But you know he always imagines himself ill, and he's quite all right really. And he's older now, and he's not tied to that mad girl he ran away with—that Miss Townsend. And besides, *I'm* older. This is probably *my* last chance!

LANDI (*calmly*): Écoute, chérie. When do you see him again?

EDITH: He's coming to tea today.

LANDI: My dear Edith, don't undertake anything yet.

EDITH: But why not?

LANDI: This may be merely an impulse—a passing mood. You may change again. Have him to tea, but give him no hope. Live for the day. Will you promise me that?

EDITH: Very well, Landi. I promise you that.

LANDI: Then we'll meet again and talk it over.

EDITH: Must I tell him nothing? Not even make him a *little* bit happy?

LANDI: Tell him nothing. Be nice to him. Enjoy your tea…. When does he come?

EDITH: He'll be here any moment.

LANDI (*jesting*): Oh—may I stay too? (*Eying* EDITH) Ah! I see I'm not wanted. But if you're not careful, Edith, *one* person *will* join you.

EDITH (*laughing*): Madame Frabelle? Oh, no, she won't!

LANDI: Good-bye, my dear. (*As he turns to go, a bell rings.*)

EDITH: Ah—that's Aylmer now! (*She dashes into the hall, where she greets* AYLMER.) Aylmer! (*The front door slams, and* EDITH *returns, followed by* AYLMER, *still walking with a cane.*)

AYLMER (*pleasantly*): Landi! (*They shake hands.*)

LANDI (*smiling*): Aylmer!

EDITH: Landi's just leaving.

LANDI (*jesting*): I asked to stay, but I see I'm not wanted. (*He kisses* EDITH *on the cheek.*) Good-bye, my dear. Good-bye, Aylmer.

AYLMER: Good-bye, Landi.

EDITH (*accompanying* LANDI *to the door*): Good-bye, dearest Landi. And thank you for coming. (LANDI *goes out; the front door slams, and* EDITH *returns.*)

AYLMER: Edith, darling. (*He takes* EDITH *in his arms and begins kissing her fingers one by one.*)

EDITH: Oh, don't, Aylmer! Please! (*Drawing away*) Tell me about Teddy.

AYLMER: Teddy! Oh—there's not much to tell. (*Laughing*) I believe he's fallen in love with Miss Clay.

EDITH: Well, no wonder. Think how pretty she is!

AYLMER: I don't think she's pretty.

EDITH: I'm trying to arrange for her to become a companion for Lady Conroy.

AYLMER: Will it be all right?

EDITH: She's to see Lady Conroy tomorrow.

AYLMER: Well, Teddy's going back on Monday anyway, and I certainly don't need a nurse any more…. (*Suddenly*) What scent do you use, Edith?

EDITH: I hardly ever use any.

AYLMER: But lately you have. And I like it.

EDITH: It's got a silly name. It's called Omar Khayyám. (*She rings the bell.*)

AYLMER: I *thought* it was Oriental. And I think *you're* Oriental.

EDITH: I believe I am—in some ways. I like lying down on cushions. I like flowers. I hate exercise and cricket and bridge.

AYLMER (*laughing*): You wouldn't care for life in a harem, would you?

EDITH: I could imagine worse things.

AYLMER: I'll take you to Egypt. You've never been there, have you?

EDITH (*her eyes sparkling*): Never!

AYLMER: I'll take you to see the Sphinx.

EDITH: Oh, Aylmer, you *are* looking well!

AYLMER: I wonder why? You don't think I'm happy, do you?

EDITH: *I* am.

AYLMER: Because you're a woman. You live for the moment.

EDITH: Oh, but you're wrong! It's not women who live for the moment.

AYLMER: I don't know that the average woman does. But then you're not the average woman.

EDITH: What am I?

AYLMER (*fatuously*): You're Edith. (*Pleased,* EDITH *moves away.*) Now, that's awfully mean of you, Edith—taking advantage of my wounded leg! (*She moves farther away.*) And that's even meaner! It's treacherous! (*She sits down; he follows her.*) Angel!

(BENNETT *enters carrying the tea tray and places it before* EDITH.)

BENNETT: Tea, ma'am.

EDITH: Oh, thank you, Bennett.

(EDITH *and* AYLMER *burst into laughter as* BENNETT *goes out.*)

CURTAIN

Scene Three

Afternoon. EDITH *and* MADAME FRABELLE *are seated on the sofa.*
MADAME FRABELLE *is knitting;* EDITH *is studying an art book.*

EDITH (*laughing*): But, Eglantine—what is the meaning of this
design? It seems to me quite unsuited to Chesterton's work—
olive-green, with twirly things on it!

MADAME FRABELLE: *I* think it rather artistic.

EDITH: It looks like macaroni—or spaghetti!

MADAME FRABELLE: Edith, darling, you're not at all—forgive
my asking—you're not the least bit restless today?

EDITH: Oh, I hope not! I believe I miss Archie a good deal.

MADAME FRABELLE: Ah, yes—I miss the dear boy immensely
myself…. Edith, dear.

EDITH: Yes?

MADAME FRABELLE: I've been wanting to tell you something.
Something—*rather* serious.

EDITH: Indeed?

MADAME FRABELLE (*continuing her knitting*): Very often when
one's living with a person, one doesn't notice little things a com-
parative stranger would observe.

EDITH: What have you observed?

MADAME FRABELLE: I've observed your husband.

EDITH: My husband?

MADAME FRABELLE: Edith, my dear, your husband's not well.

EDITH: Oh, I'm sorry you think that!

MADAME FRABELLE (*as if announcing a great discovery*): He suffers, my dear Edith, from nerves.

EDITH (*smiling*): Who should know that better than I?

MADAME FRABELLE: He's terribly depressed. He says things to
me that—well, that really quite alarm me.

EDITH: You mustn't take Bruce too seriously, my dear.

Madame Frabelle: I *don't* take him too seriously! And I've done my best either to change the subject or to make him see the silver lining to every cloud.

Edith: I think what Bruce needs is a silver lining to his *purse*.

Madame Frabelle: You're jesting, Edith, dear!

Edith: Bruce worries about money.

Madame Frabelle: But only incidentally. Mr. Ottley is really worried about the war.

Edith: I suppose we all are.

Madame Frabelle: But Mr. Ottley takes it particularly to heart.

Edith: "Mr. Ottley." Why suddenly this distant manner, Eglantine? I thought you always called him Bruce.

Madame Frabelle: I do, of course. But don't you see, Edith, his depression is growing worse and worse.

Edith: Take care, dear—you're losing your wool. (*She gets up, walks to the other end of the room, rearranges some flowers, and returns to the sofa.*) Yes—perhaps Bruce *is* worse. He might be better if he occupied his mind more.

Madame Frabelle: He works at the Foreign Office from ten till four every day. He looks in at his club, where they talk over the news of the war. And then he comes home and we discuss it again. Really, Edith, I scarcely see how much more he could do!

Edith: But don't you see all the time he isn't *doing* anything! Anything about the war, I mean. You and I do our little best to help. But what does Bruce do? Nothing—except talk.

Madame Frabelle: That's just it, Edith! I doubt if your husband is fit for any more work than he does already. He's not strong, you know.

Edith: Of course I know. If he were strong he wouldn't be here.

Madame Frabelle: What was it exactly that prevented his joining?

Edith (*trying to keep her voice perfectly natural*): Neurotic heart.

Madame Frabelle: Ah! Ah! That must cause him a great deal of pain. But I think his worst symptoms are his nervous fears.

Look at last night. (*She puts down her knitting and folds it into her workbasket.*)

EDITH: Last night?

MADAME FRABELLE: Last night, because there was no moon, and it wasn't raining, and it was fairly clear, Mr. Ott— Bruce absolutely made up his mind there'd be a Zeppelin raid. Well, instead of being satisfied when I told him I'd got out my mask, and left the bath half filled with water, and helped put two large bags of sand outside his dressing-room door—in spite of all that, do you know what happened in the middle of the night?

EDITH: I'm afraid I don't.

MADAME FRABELLE: Well, at three o'clock in the morning, fancy my surprise to hear a knock at my door!

EDITH: I wonder I didn't hear a knock at *mine.*

MADAME FRABELLE: Your husband was afraid to disturb you! Most considerate, *I* thought.

EDITH: *Most* considerate.

MADAME FRABELLE: Well, he knocked at my door and said he was unable to sleep, was utterly wretched, and felt like cutting his throat.

EDITH: Cutting his throat!

MADAME FRABELLE: Oh, I don't think he really *meant* it.

EDITH: But what a shame to disturb *you!*

MADAME FRABELLE: I didn't mind in the least. I was only too pleased. So what do you think I did?

EDITH: I can't think *what* you did.

MADAME FRABELLE: I got up and dressed, went down to the library and lighted the fire, and sat up half an hour with your husband trying to cheer him up.

EDITH: That was very sweet of you, Eglantine.

MADAME FRABELLE: I made a cup of tea, Bruce had a whisky and soda, we had a nice talk, and I sent him back to bed.

EDITH (*laughing*): Rather hard on *you,* Eglantine, wasn't it!

(BENNETT *enters carrying the tea tray, places it on a table near* MADAME FRABELLE, *and goes out.*)

MADAME FRABELLE: Not at all, dear! Not at all! If I can only feel I've done a *little* good during my stay here, I shall be quite satisfied.

EDITH: Oh, but you mustn't dream yet of *going!*

(BRUCE *appears at the door.*)

MADAME FRABELLE: Why, here's Mr. Ottley—just in time for tea!

BRUCE: Oh, hallo, Edith.

EDITH: How are you feeling, Bruce?

BRUCE (*sighing*): Oh, pretty rotten. I had a very bad night. How are *you* feeling, Madame Frabelle?

MADAME FRABELLE: Oh, very well, thank you, Mr. Ottley. Tea? (*Handing* BRUCE *a cup*) I've been telling Edith—

BRUCE (*suddenly tense*): What have you been telling Edith?

MADAME FRABELLE: About last night.

BRUCE: You can't think how kind she was to me, Edith.

EDITH: I'm sure she *was!*

MADAME FRABELLE (*cheerily*): Oh, you won't have a bad night like *that* again!

BRUCE: If it hadn't been for her, I don't know what I'd have done…. Oh, by the way, Edith, how's Aylmer?

EDITH: Aylmer? I believe he's been ordered out of town.

BRUCE: For God's sake, don't let him go to the east coast!

MADAME FRABELLE: The east coast is quite as safe as any other part of England.

BRUCE: I expect he'll miss *you,* Edith. You've been so jolly good to him lately.

MADAME FRABELLE (*a bit too quickly*): Naturally! Naturally! Anyone so kindhearted as Edith would be sure to try and cheer up the convalescence of a wounded friend. (*To* EDITH) Have a *foie-gras* sandwich?

BRUCE: We're all fond of old Aylmer, you know.

MADAME FRABELLE: I know. I know. And I quite understand. You're great friends. (*With an air of scrupulous justice*) Personally, I think Mr. Ross has behaved splendidly.

BRUCE: You don't care for him, I fancy.

MADAME FRABELLE: Oh, I won't say *that*. I admit there's a certain coldness, a certain hard reserve about his character that— Well, frankly it doesn't appeal to *me*. But I always hope to be fair. He's a man I *respect*.

BRUCE: But he doesn't amuse you—what?

MADAME FRABELLE: The fact is—he has no sense of humour.

BRUCE: Oh, really? *I* call him a good-natured sort of chap. You never find Aylmer depressed.

MADAME FRABELLE: No, not depressed. But he hasn't got— You won't be angry with me for what I say, will you?

BRUCE: Not at all!

MADAME FRABELLE: You won't be cross with me, Edith?

EDITH: Oh, do go on!

MADAME FRABELLE: Well, in *my* opinion Aylmer Ross has brains, but no temperament.

BRUCE: Precisely! Brains, but no temperament.

MADAME FRABELLE: Mind you, that doesn't prevent his being an excellent soldier.

BRUCE: Oh, dear, no! He's done jolly well at the front. But, Edith, I think I know what she means.

EDITH: I'm sure *she* knows…. I don't quite understand what people mean when they say other people have no temperament. What *is* temperament?

MADAME FRABELLE: Oh, my dear, it's a sort of—a sort of *atmosphere*. It's what I might call the magnetism of personality.

BRUCE: Precisely! The magnetism of personality.

EDITH: But isn't Aylmer said to be rather generous?

BRUCE: Oh, yes—he's quite generous. I've known him to do ever so many kind things and never let a soul except the fellow he'd helped know anything about it.

MADAME FRABELLE: I don't doubt for a moment he's a generous man. But he has the effect on me—

EDITH: Go on, Eglantine.

MADAME FRABELLE: Frankly, he chills me to the bone. When I went to see him with Edith, I felt more tired after a quarter of an hour's talk with him than I would— (*She glances at* BRUCE.)

EDITH: Than you would after *three* hours' talk with Bruce.

MADAME FRABELLE: That's what I mean! He's difficult to talk to!

EDITH: I have no doubt you're right.

BRUCE: Well, she generally is. She's so infernally deep sometimes, she sees things nobody else would suspect.

MADAME FRABELLE (*pleased*): Oh, *do* I?

EDITH: You do indeed. (*Rising*) You won't think it horrid of me, Bruce, if I go out for a few minutes?

BRUCE: Oh, no, no, no! Certainly not. Do go, my dear girl. You'll be back to dinner? (*He rises.*)

EDITH: Of course. It isn't a quarter to six. I quite forgot something I promised to do. For Mrs. Mitchell.

(BRUCE *goes out.*)

MADAME FRABELLE (*archly*): Ah—Mrs. Mitchell. *I* know what it is! It's that Society for the Belgians. (*She rises.*)

EDITH: That's it exactly. Well, I'll fly—and be back as soon as I can.

MADAME FRABELLE: Of course. Of course. For heaven's sake, Edith, don't treat *me* with ceremony! (*She goes out just as* BENNETT *enters.*)

BENNETT (*announcing*): Mr. Aylmer Ross!

(AYLMER *enters;* BENNETT *goes out.*)

EDITH: Aylmer, darling! You're walking without your cane!

AYLMER: For the first time.

EDITH: I'm so glad you could come—if only for a moment. I was just coming to *you.*

AYLMER (*kissing* EDITH*'s hand*): Angel!

EDITH: Bruce is too irritating for words today. And Madame Frabelle makes me sick.

AYLMER (*laughing*): *You're* not jealous of Madame Frabelle!

EDITH: Good heavens, no! But she has such a pompous way of discovering the obvious.

AYLMER: I do believe you object to her being in love with Bruce.

EDITH: But she's *not* in love with Bruce! Who *could* be?

AYLMER: You're using that Omar Khayyám scent again. I wish you wouldn't.

EDITH: But you said you liked it!

AYLMER: I like it too much.

EDITH: Oh, Aylmer—how strange you are!

AYLMER: I can't do that sort of thing, Edith. I can't. Once you've given me your promise—yes. But not before.

EDITH: Oh, Aylmer!

AYLMER: I won't rush you, dear. In time you'll see I'm right.

EDITH: You don't love me!

AYLMER: I *do* love you…. And now I must go.

EDITH: Oh, Aylmer—are you really leaving town?

AYLMER: I'm *ordered* to leave. But I doubt if I can stand it.

EDITH: Well, good-bye, Aylmer, dear.

AYLMER: Are you sending me away already?

EDITH: Why, Aylmer—you've just said you must go!

AYLMER: I can stand talking with you for hours, Edith. But I can't stand being within a yard of you for ten seconds.

EDITH (*laughing*): Thank you so much!

AYLMER: How often must I tell you, Edith?

EDITH: Tell me what?

AYLMER: I'm not that sort of man.

EDITH: What sort?

AYLMER: I can't kiss people.

EDITH: I'm very glad you can't. I'd hate you to kiss *people*.

AYLMER: I can't do those things, Edith.

EDITH: Oh, Aylmer!

(*They go out arm-in-arm.*)

CURTAIN

Scene Four

Morning. EDITH *and* BRUCE *are seated at the breakfast table.* BRUCE *is reading a newspaper;* EDITH *is reading a letter.*

EDITH: Oh, Bruce—I've just had a letter from Aylmer—from Eastcliff.

BRUCE (*from behind his newspaper*): Got him off to the seaside, have they?

EDITH: He finds it frightfully dull. He's bored.

BRUCE (*putting down his newspaper*): I daresay he is. I'm sure *I'd* feel half inclined to cut my throat if I were alone, with a game leg, at a place like that.

EDITH: But he's much better, and he's going back to the front in a fortnight.

BRUCE: In a fortnight! Pretty sharp work!

EDITH: He's counting the hours till he can get away.

BRUCE: Jolly good fellow, Aylmer.

EDITH: I wonder if you'd mind, Bruce, if I went down for the day to see him?

BRUCE: Mind! Oh, *dear,* no! I think it's your duty. Poor old chap—I wonder you don't run down for the weekend.

EDITH: Well, I *might* go down tomorrow for a couple of days.

BRUCE: Do!

EDITH: Wouldn't you miss me, now that Archie's at school?

BRUCE: Not at bit!

EDITH: Wouldn't the house seem very quiet?

BRUCE: Not the least bit! I *long* for quiet. You don't half understand my condition, Edith. The quieter I am, the better.

EDITH: But wouldn't it seem the least bit rude to Madame Frabelle? She talks of going away soon.

BRUCE: Oh, *she* won't mind. We never treat *her* with ceremony.

(MADAME FRABELLE *enters.*)

MADAME FRABELLE: Oh, Edith, dear—has anyone seen my spectacles? I think I must have left them— (*Suddenly she sees them on the table.*) Ah, there they are! (*She gives a nervous little laugh, picks up the spectacles, and starts to go.*) Do you know, Edith—I'm half expecting a telegram which *may* take me away.

EDITH: Take you away?

MADAME FRABELLE: I have a relative who's anxious for me to go and stay with her.

EDITH: Oh, really?

MADAME FRABELLE: An old aunt. She's very, very old, and very, very— But even if I do go away, perhaps you'd let me come back to you after?

EDITH: Why, yes, my dear—of course!

MADAME FRABELLE: Thank you, dear Edith. You're a kind, sweet friend. (*She goes out.*)

BRUCE (*pleasantly*): Who knows, Edith? Perhaps we'll never meet again.

EDITH: You and Eglantine?

BRUCE: You and I. Perhaps the Zeppelins will come while you're away. Perhaps they'll set fire to your hotel in Eastcliff!

EDITH: Well, if you want me, Bruce, you've only to telephone, and I can be back in an hour.

(BENNETT *enters.*)

BENNETT (*announcing*): Mr. Aylmer Ross!

(AYLMER *enters;* BENNETT *goes out.*)

EDITH (*astonished*): Aylmer!

BRUCE (*cordially*): Aylmer, old chap!

EDITH: But—Aylmer! We've just this moment—

AYLMER: I'm here for two days. I suddenly got leave.

EDITH: Two days…. *What* a surprise!

BRUCE (*slapping* AYLMER *heartily on the shoulder*): Well, you're always welcome, old boy. Always welcome. (*Starting to go*) Aylmer, old chap—will you forgive me if I leave you to my wife?

AYLMER: Certainly, my dear fellow!

BRUCE: A bit of business, you know. A bit of business. (*At the door*) You *will* forgive me?

AYLMER: Of course, Bruce.

BRUCE: Take care of him, Edith!

EDITH: Of course, Bruce.

(BRUCE *goes out.*)

AYLMER: Edith, darling! I've been counting the minutes.

EDITH (*joyous*): Oh, Aylmer!

AYLMER: Well, Edith, are you ready to put me out of suspense? It'll be jolly to have two days' leave in London, but it'll be far from jolly if you don't give me that promise.

EDITH: But doesn't the promise refer to after you come back?

AYLMER: I don't ask you to come away with me till I'm back again. But I want you to promise before that you will.

EDITH (*firmly*): Well, Aylmer, I promise. I'm ready to promise. I mean to do it.

AYLMER (*ecstatic*): At last! You mean to do it! Oh, Edith, I've been waiting for you for four years—ever since that night I met you at the Mitchells'.

EDITH: Oh, Aylmer—we'll never be happier than we are right now.

AYLMER: Rubbish! What about our life when I come back? Every dream realized!

EDITH: And yet you're going out again to risk it.

AYLMER: Don't you worry. I'll come back like a bad penny!… Edith, dear, say you mean it—say it *again*.

EDITH: Say I mean what?

AYLMER: Say you love me. Say you'll marry me. Say you and Archie will belong to me. You won't have any regrets?

EDITH: I won't have any regrets.

AYLMER: Swear you won't have any regrets.

EDITH: Most women know what they want till they get it, and then they want something else. But when *I* get what I want I don't regret it.

AYLMER: But, Edith—to think this might have happened four years ago!

EDITH: But then I *would* have had regrets.

AYLMER: I'd have made you forget them soon enough.

EDITH: Aylmer, how can I bear your going out again? All we've gone through may be for nothing!

AYLMER: Now that I have your promise, everything will be all right. And look here, Edith—you needn't be unhappy about Bruce. We'll tell him everything when I come back.

EDITH: But suppose—you *don't* come back.

AYLMER: Dearest Edith, I must go. (*Checking his watch*) I must appear before the board at eleven o'clock.

EDITH: One kiss?

AYLMER: Dear girl, I've told you a thousand times it's a thing I can't do.

EDITH: But, Aylmer, darling—we're engaged!

AYLMER: Of course we're engaged!

EDITH: Then is it wrong for you to kiss your fiancée?

AYLMER: Of course it's not wrong! Only—I can't! I haven't the self-command.

EDITH: Oh, Aylmer!

AYLMER: Good-bye, my darling.

(EDITH *accompanies* AYLMER *to the door. As she returns,* BENNETT *appears in the hall.*)

EDITH: Oh, Bennett—have you seen Madame Frabelle?

BENNETT: She's gone away, ma'am.

EDITH (*astonished*): Gone away! What do you mean?

BENNETT: She's gone away, ma'am.

EDITH: Gone away—without seeing *me?*

BENNETT: She left this letter for you, ma'am. (*She hands the letter to* EDITH.)

EDITH: Thank you, Bennett. That will be all. (BENNETT *goes out.* EDITH *opens the letter and reads.*) "My dearest Edith, To my great regret a telegram I half expected has come, and I'm compelled to leave for Liverpool to join my aunt, who is very ill. I'll write again and give you my address.

"May I say one word? I fear your husband is very unwell indeed. His nerves are in a terrible state, and I think his condition is more serious than you suppose. He should be humoured in everything. I say this for your own good."

(BENNETT *enters*.)

BENNETT (*announcing*): Sir Tito Landi!

(LANDI *enters*; BENNETT *goes out*.)

EDITH: Oh, Landi, my dear! You always come just when I need you most!

LANDI: Edith, *ma chère*. I've only a moment.

EDITH: I've just had a letter from Madame Frabelle.

LANDI: *Eh bien—La Mère Frabelle! La vieille qui voit double!* And where is Madame Frabelle?

EDITH: Apparently she's on her way to Liverpool.

LANDI: Liverpool!

EDITH: She says she'll write. Here—read her letter. (*She hands the letter to* LANDI.)

LANDI: Ah…. Ah…. (*Reading*) "Never think me wanting in gratitude and friendship. Truly I am still your affectionate friend, Eglantine."

EDITH: How like her to lay down the law about Bruce!

LANDI: When does Aylmer return to the front?

EDITH: He goes before the board this morning.

LANDI: And you've had your talk?

EDITH: We've had our talk. I've made my promise. I've told him I mean to do it. *After* he returns from the front.

LANDI: Oh, good—good! I'm much relieved. Now you'll have nothing on your conscience *before*.

(BRUCE *enters, looking pale and depressed*.)

BRUCE: Oh, hallo, Edith. Hallo, Landi. Very bad news in the morning papers.

EDITH: Very bad news?

BRUCE: Very bad.

LANDI (*going*): Good-bye, Edith, my dear. I must be off. (*He kisses* EDITH *on the cheek.*) Good-bye, Bruce.

BRUCE: Good-bye, Landi.

EDITH (*accompanying* LANDI *to the door*): Thank you, my dear. Thank you for everything.

(LANDI *goes out. The front door slams, and* EDITH *returns.*)

BRUCE: Edith, I have something to say to you.

EDITH: To me?

BRUCE: Something—very serious.

EDITH: Yes, Bruce?

BRUCE (*abruptly*): Good heavens, Edith! If I've spoken of it once, I've spoken of it forty times! That inkstand is still too full!

EDITH: Oh, Bruce—I'm dreadfully sorry!

BRUCE: Edith, I wish to tell you something.

EDITH: What is it, Bruce?

BRUCE (*hesitating*): Edith, I'm—I'm in a strange state of health. I find I can no longer bear living in London. If I'm to keep sane, if I'm not to commit suicide, I must give up this domestic life…. I'm—I'm going away.

EDITH (*calmly*): Going away?

BRUCE: I'm going to America.

EDITH: America!

BRUCE: I've already taken my passage. I thought of leaving without telling you, but I decided it was better to be open.

EDITH: You mean you're going to America on a trip?

BRUCE: No, Edith. I can't endure married life any longer. Four years ago I offered you your freedom and you refused to take it. I offer it again today.

EDITH: You mean to leave us altogether then?

BRUCE: That's just what I mean.

EDITH: But will you be happy—comfortable—alone in America?

BRUCE: Edith, I'm sorry to pain you, but I'll not be alone.

EDITH: What do you mean? Is Madame Frabelle—?

BRUCE: Edith, I'll not deny it. We mean to throw in our lot together.

EDITH (*calmly*): I see.

BRUCE: Of course I give up the Foreign Office and my salary there. But you have some money of your own, Edith. It'll be enough for you and Archie to live quietly.

EDITH: You mean to get something to do?

BRUCE: Yes—when I'm strong enough.

EDITH (*kindly*): Have you any fault to find with me, Bruce?

BRUCE: Edith, you're a perfect mother. And I've no fault to find with you as a wife. But I'm not happy here. I'm miserable. I implore you not to make a scene. Don't oppose me. Forgive me—on account of my health.

EDITH (*decisively*): Bruce—I'll not make a scene. I'll not oppose you. I'll do exactly as you wish. And I hope you'll be happy and well.

BRUCE (*abruptly, seeing* EDITH *move near the writing table*): Look out, Edith! You'll have that inkstand over!

EDITH (*laughing hysterically*): Oh, Bruce!

BRUCE: You won't mind, Edith, if I go down to the club for an hour?

EDITH: Certainly not, Bruce.

BRUCE: And, Edith—say what you can to my mother. Tell her it's to save my going off my head.

EDITH: I will, Bruce.

BRUCE: I've taken a room at the club. I'll send up for my luggage.

EDITH: Would you like to see Archie before you go?

BRUCE: Edith, I'd better not. I don't think my nerves would stand it.

EDITH: Very well, Bruce.

BRUCE: Try not to be angry, Edith. Perhaps some day—

EDITH (*firmly*): No. Never.

BRUCE: You'd never let me come back to see you?

EDITH: Never. Never.

BRUCE: Edith?

EDITH: Yes, Bruce?

BRUCE: Oh—nothing. (*Going*) You needn't be so cross, Edith. Remember my health.

EDITH: I do, Bruce.

BRUCE: And—Edith?

EDITH: Yes, Bruce?

BRUCE: Don't forget about that inkstand. It's always filled just a little too full. (*At the door*) You *will* remember?

EDITH: Yes, Bruce—I'll remember.

BRUCE: Good-bye, Edith.

EDITH: Good-bye, Bruce.

(BENNETT *enters.*)

BENNETT (*announcing*): Mr. Aylmer Ross!

(AYLMER *enters;* BENNETT *goes out.*)

BRUCE (*casually*): Oh, hallo, Aylmer.

AYLMER: Hello, Bruce.

BRUCE: I'm just going.

AYLMER: Going?

BRUCE: Good-bye, Aylmer.

(BRUCE *and* AYLMER *shake hands.* BRUCE *goes out.* EDITH *rushes into* AYLMER*'s arms.*)

EDITH: Oh, Aylmer, darling!

AYLMER: Edith, dearest. I'm not going away after all!

EDITH: Not going away?

AYLMER: They won't have me! They've given me an appointment at the War Office.

EDITH: Oh, Aylmer! How wonderful! I couldn't have borne your going out again.

AYLMER: Dearest Edith.

EDITH: And now, Aylmer, I needn't keep my promise.

AYLMER: What on earth do you mean?

EDITH: Bruce wants to leave me. He's deserting me. He's deserting Archie too.

AYLMER: Edith! Do you mean—?

EDITH: Bruce is gone! Bruce is really gone!

AYLMER: Do you mean—like before?

EDITH: Yes. Only this time he won't be coming back.

AYLMER: Ah!

EDITH: And this time he wants me to divorce him.

AYLMER: Ah!

EDITH: And this time—I will!

AYLMER: Edith! Do you mean he'll marry again?

EDITH: Of course! And *she'll* take care of him. He'll be all right!

AYLMER: Oh, Edith! Thank heaven for Madame Frabelle!

EDITH: Thank heaven for Madame Frabelle!

(EDITH *is back in* AYLMER*'s arms; he kisses her passionately.*)

CURTAIN

A Note on the Author

ROBERT MANSON MYERS, educator, historian, playwright, and literary critic, is Professor of English Emeritus at the University of Maryland. He graduated *summa cum laude* from Vanderbilt University and received graduate degrees from Columbia University and Harvard University. After teaching at Yale University, The College of William and Mary, and Tulane University, he was Fulbright Research Scholar at The University of London and Fulbright Visiting Professor at The University of Rotterdam.

Dr. Myers's plays have been staged on both sides of the Atlantic and aired on the BBC. His numerous books include two works on the composer Handel and the classic spoof, *From Beowulf to Virginia Woolf: An Astounding and Wholly Unauthorized History of English Literature.* His best-selling Civil War epic, *The Children of Pride,* widely acclaimed as "The American *War and Peace,*" won the coveted Carey-Thomas Award in 1972 and the prestigious National Book Award in 1973.